THE ILLUSTRATOR'S GUIDE

THE ILLUSTRATOR'S GUIDE

How to create an exceptional freelance illustration career

James Hughes

The Illustrator's Guide: How to create an exceptional freelance career

ISBN: 978-1-7395578-1-2 (Hardback edition)
ISBN: 978-1-3999-6267-4 (Paperback edition)
ISBN: 978-1-7395578-0-5 (eBook)

British Library Cataloguing-in-Publication data
A catalogue record for this book is available from the British Library

Library of Congress Cataloging-in-Publication data
A catalog record for this book is available from the Library of Congress

The purpose of this book is to provide the reader with general information about the subject matter presented. This book is not intended, nor should the user consider it, to be legal advice for a specific situation.

The author, company and publisher make no representations or warranties with respect to the accuracy, fitness, completeness or applicability of the contents of this book. The author, company and publisher shall in no event be held liable for any loss or other damages, including but not limited to special, incidental, consequential, or other damages. Please consider carefully any advice the author gives before applying it in your workplace.

Cover design: Tom Etherington
Design: James Hughes
Illustration: Michael Parkin

Typeset in Times New Roman & Proxima Nova

Contents

Introduction   1

Chapter 1: How to develop an exceptional mindset   5

It's okay to be a beginner   5
Everybody starts somewhere   5
Commit to the craft   7
You get out what you put in   8
Expand your skill set   9

Chapter 2: Facing challenges and overcoming barriers   11

Do you feel like an impostor?   11
Getting over impostor syndrome   11
The confidence conundrum   13
Fear of rejection   14
Comparing your work to other illustrators   17
Rehearse scenarios and prepare scripts   18
Be persistent   20
Competing for work   21
How to be lucky   21
Skill is worth more than talent   22
Don't find your passion, build it   22

Chapter 3: Your start-up essentials   25

What's essential   25
What's not essential   26
Better kit doesn't make a better illustrator   27
Prioritise your time   27
Protect your time   29
Stick to a schedule   33
How to set yourself up for a good day's work   33
Get to work   36
Short-term pain for long-term gain   37
Your portfolio doesn't need to be perfect   39
What to include   39

Chapter 4: Developing your portfolio 39

Why are you including it? 40
Your portfolio jigsaw puzzle 42
Who are your illustrations for? 44
What do your illustrations do? 46
Curate your portfolio 47
How to identify a commercial style 49
Why unique illustration styles sell 51
You have to start to be great 53
Celebrate your mistakes 53

Chapter 5: Forming and maintaining your creative habit 54

Your first clients are for motivation 55
Small steps in the right direction 55
Setting goals 58
Planning your next steps 60
Quick wins 61
Online learning platforms 62
Don't wait for inspiration 64
A great portfolio takes time 67

Chapter 6: Practice makes progress 67

Practise deliberately 68
Learning by copying 70
Adding something only you can do 70
What if you're being copied? 71
Embrace your influences 72
Productive procrastination 72
Grow your illustration community 74

Chapter 7: Get feedback on your work 77

Why an outside perspective is important 77
When to get feedback 77
Where to get feedback 80
Not all advice is good advice 82
The more feedback, the better 84
Responding to feedback 84
Dealing with difficult feedback 85
Don't take it personally 86
Reflect on your own performance 87
Prospecting for new clients never stops 93
Who is your client? 93

Chapter 8: How to find clients — 93

Finding and researching clients — 94
Build up a client list — 96
Be open to all opportunities — 97
Find those contact details — 98
Follow up on your introductory emails — 99
Why clients don't respond — 100
Give the client a reason to respond — 101
Keep in touch with clients long-term — 101
Build trust with clients — 102

Chapter 9: Working with clients — 105

Solve problems, don't create them — 105
Your first commissions — 106
Doing the job — 109
Why the process works this way — 110
Managing expectations — 111
Delivery — 112
Make a good impression to get referrals — 113
Good clients versus bad clients — 114
Win better clients — 117

Chapter 10: How to deal with client briefs — 119

What is a brief? — 119
Briefs come in all shapes and sizes — 126
Ask lots of questions — 126
Calls and video chats with clients — 127
Using your money wisely — 133
Don't spend before you're earning — 133

Chapter 11: Managing your money — 133

Quick and cheap self-promotion — 134
When to quit the day job — 135
Working for free — 137
How to make more money — 141

Chapter 12: A freelancer is a business — 143

Building your freelance business — 143
Communicate effectively — 145
Be your own salesperson — 146
Offer your expertise — 147
What makes a professional — 148

Chapter 13: Pricing your work and negotiating 151

Treat pricing as an experiment 151
Your personal pricing guide 152
Low price equals low value 154
Price appropriately to your level 155
Aim for the ballpark 155
Value versus cost 156
What kind of client is it? 158
Negotiating 158
There's always time to think about your price 161
Offer high value and charge a high price 162

Chapter 14: Licensing, rights and contracts 164

Non-disclosure agreements 165
Licensing your work 167
What makes a licence? 168
Copyright basics 170
Selling the rights to your work 172
Contract essentials 173
What makes a contract? 174
Other clauses to look out for 175
Insurance 177
Get it in writing 177

Chapter 15: Finding an agent 179

The benefits of working with an agent 179
What an agent can do for you 180
What an agent can't do 182
What does an agency look for? 182
When to approach an agent 185
Submit your work the right way 186
Introducing yourself to an agency 187
Choosing an agency 190
After signing with an agent 193

Chapter 16: Working with an agent   195

Your agent is your business partner   195
Outsourcing work to an agent   195
How agents get you work   196
How agents are paid   197
Agents solve problems   197
Agents are human   198
Work harder than your agent   198
Build the relationship with your agent   200
Give a lot and expect a lot   200
Trust each other   201

Final thoughts   203

Further resources   207

Acknowledgements   213

About the author   215

Introduction

Imagine the thrill of walking into a bookshop and finding your work bringing words to life, or seeing your illustrations advertising the world's most prestigious brands. Illustration offers you, as a skilled artist, endless opportunities to captivate, motivate and educate audiences of all ages and backgrounds.

As a skilled illustrator, not only can you make an excellent living from your art, but you have the freedom to steer your career in whatever direction you want. You can gain respect and recognition by doing something you genuinely enjoy. Illustration is a fascinating career to talk about and share with others too – if you can't be an astronaut or rock star, being an illustrator is pretty close (in my book, anyway!).

Now more than ever, an illustrator who wants these things – and a long, sustainable career – must focus on becoming outstanding at what they do. Clients are becoming less interested in ordinary illustrators producing average work. The competition from other creatives is fiercer than ever: there will always be people who undercut your price. Additionally, stock illustrations provide a quick and convenient alternative, and AI technology offers clients who don't value human creativity a new and inexpensive way to source images for their projects.[1]

Despite these challenges, there are still many exceptional and remarkable illustrators dedicated to their craft: they've fought their way through the competition and come out the other side successfully. They have the opportunity to collaborate with clients who pay a lot of money for outstanding work. While the value of low-quality illustration falls in a saturated market, illustration that stands out from the crowd becomes increasingly valuable – it's never been more important to be exceptional.

It takes time to battle your way through the low-quality competition, but it's worth the effort.

---

1   At the time of writing, issues regarding generative AI's place in the creative world, and its impact on artists' intellectual property, are still undecided.

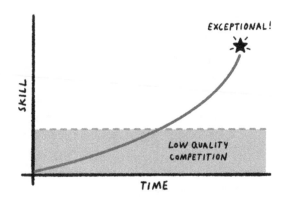

The best clients want to work with the best creatives, so if you want to collaborate with them, you need something extraordinary to offer. This book explores what makes an exceptional illustrator, and gives you a clear path to get there.

Who this book is for

If you hope to make freelance illustration your career, this book is for you. It's for new illustrators who:

- Are committed to developing their skills
- Want to offer the world something outstanding
- Have the drive to push themselves towards a rewarding and fulfilling career.

Whether you're just starting out or in the early years of your illustration journey, this book provides you with all the tools and insights to help you become a confident professional. The time it takes to get there can vary from person to person, but the expert information and guidance in these pages will help you get there faster.

Why should you listen to me?

In 2010 I set out to become a freelance illustrator, inspired by my heroes in the industry. I idolised illustrators like Jasper Goodall, Steve

Scott and Vault 49, their work seemed to be everywhere I looked. They were our sector's superstars, and I wanted what they had: respect, fame and a deeply cool job (and not least, their kind of hard-earned skills too).

As time went by, I realised I liked the *idea* of being an illustrator more than I liked the actual process of *becoming* one – being creative on demand wasn't for me. I found myself drawn to connecting talented creatives with exciting projects, and helping others achieve their creative ambitions.

Now I'm privileged to work with truly skilled and dedicated illustrators as an agent. I see commercial artists at the top of their game, working on an unbelievable range of projects every day. They're today's illustration superstars, and they've shown me that it's not just a fun job for them – or about fame or recognition.

It's about the craft.

These illustrators have dedicated themselves to the process of perfecting their skills, so they can offer something remarkable and beautiful to the world. They've taught me what it takes to excel in a creative career.

This book shares those insights with you.

My experience of freelance illustration, combined with the skills and knowledge I've gained as an agent, have equipped me to support, guide and advise illustrators at all stages of their careers. My blog and YouTube channel, *The Illustrator's Guide,*[2] have helped many aspiring illustrators find answers to industry-related questions and navigate the challenges they encounter on their journey to becoming professionals.

Just as importantly (if not more so), my experiences as an illustrator and agent have taught me what not to do. I've seen the good and the bad; I've been rejected and inspired.

This book will help you avoid common traps and focus your attention on what truly matters.

What this book will do for you

We're going to start by taking a look at the mindset required to start up a creative career, breaking down some of the mental barriers and challenges you might face as a new illustrator. Then we'll consider the shortest route from beginner to professional illustrator, including:

- What to focus your time on
- How to develop a portfolio that gets you hired
- How to build your creative habit.

We'll look at how to seek out feedback on your work to make it the best it can be, then dive into how to find clients, discussing everything you can expect from illustration commissions.

We'll work on developing your new freelance business and answer some questions on pricing and negotiating, then we'll get into everything you need to know about copyright, licensing and contracts.

Finally, we'll discuss the pros and cons of working with an agent and how you can go about getting one, if that's the way you want to go.

You'll find this book filled with top tips, exercises and practical, step-by-step advice to help you become that exceptional freelance illustrator.

Now you know what to expect, let's get started!

1

How to develop an exceptional mindset

It's okay to be a beginner

I love being a beginner so much that I hope I never think of myself as an expert in anything. The more I understand about a subject or skill, the more I realise how much there is left to uncover: if I thought there were nothing left to learn, I'd be bored! Writing this book has been an excellent opportunity to reflect on what I've discovered so far, and to think about all the things I'm yet to find. I'm more interested and motivated to explore new ideas than ever.

Beginners are open-minded, curious and listen to other people without prejudgement. They aren't stuck in their ways, and they want to understand and improve. These traits are crucial for picking up new skills and, ideally, will be right at the core of how you approach your work throughout your career – not least because it'll keep things interesting and fun for you.

Keeping a beginner's mindset means you still want to improve, even when you reach an advanced level: if you stay this way, you'll always be open to growing and building on your skills. But the more experienced we become, the more difficult it can be to keep hold of these beginner's traits. Someone who considers themselves an expert could become less open to new ideas and ways of doing things, and they're going to be a lot less engaged if they stop learning.

Everybody starts somewhere

As a new illustrator, you shouldn't feel inferior just because you haven't been in the industry for long. Before your favourite illustrators were successful, they were struggling to make money, nervous about talking to clients, trying to get noticed and making plenty of mistakes – and they were almost certainly doing underpaid work too. They might even have considered giving up at various points, but they stuck with it. They showed up, put in the time and effort, worked hard and overcame setbacks. (We'll be looking at some common challenges you might face as a new illustrator, and how to overcome them, in Chapter 2.)

These experienced professionals are no different – and they're definitely not perfect – just a few steps ahead. They succeeded because they kept improving, and the best ones still do. Learning from people more experienced than us means we can improve faster as a result: there's as much to gain from their setbacks as their successes. If you stay curious enough to keep improving, you have a hell of an advantage.

When you're studying illustration in college, your teachers show interest in your work. They look at it carefully, give you feedback and guide you – it's their job to do that. But in the early days of your career, once you get out into the freelance world, you'll find that fewer people are willing to help you with your work – for a while, nobody cares about that except you. That can be tough to deal with, but it's actually a gift, because you can experiment and make mistakes without anyone paying attention. (In Chapter 7, we'll dive into the importance of feedback on your portfolio, and how you can go about getting it.)

Once you start getting paid to be an illustrator and gain followers and fans, people will be watching. Try to enjoy the freedom that being a beginner allows, and make the most of your anonymity. Experiment and take creative risks, then put what you discover to good use. There's nothing wrong with being a beginner: in fact, the industry needs new talent to show up and take chances!

You'll face frustration and setbacks – just as any new business owner does – and you might feel out of your depth while you're developing new skills; progress might not be as fast as you'd like.

But being perfect isn't the goal. What's more important is to keep improving, and that you enjoy the journey.

Commit to the craft

Establishing yourself as a freelance illustrator is a long game: it takes commitment, just as anything really worth doing does. Only a few aspiring illustrators become successful professionals; even fewer become the most sought-after and famous.

Many people who set out to be the best at something will give up somewhere along the way: not everyone has the dedication, perseverance (and possibly a bit of obsession) required to get there. Meanwhile, others might move on to something else, either out of financial necessity or because they've discovered something more important to them.

The ones who stick it out and become the best are rare outliers – which makes their work and skills highly valuable.

Of course, the top performers in any field work hard consistently for a long time. At the extreme, Olympic gold medallists show up, train every day and say 'No' to activities that don't help them achieve their goals. Concert pianists, fighter pilots, prima ballerinas and ultimate fighting champions have a single-minded focus: putting their goal above everything else.

Illustration isn't as intense as all that, but it is competitive (we'll look at this environment in more detail in the next chapter). Even if you don't aspire to be the best in the world at what you do for a job, why not aim high and see how far you can go? Aiming high and not quite hitting the target is far better than aiming low and hitting it.

Obviously, you don't need me (or indeed anyone else) to tell you that being exceptional at anything requires consistent effort – it goes without saying! Even the naturally gifted have to put in the time, stay motivated and pick themselves up after setbacks. How this impacts you as a creative freelancer is that you have two main roles: worker and boss. If the worker doesn't show up to work or misses a deadline, you can be sure the boss will have something to say about it. And if the boss doesn't encourage, motivate and hold the worker accountable, nothing will get done.

Looking to achieve long-term success as an illustrator means being a self-starter. If you're unenthusiastic about becoming the best option for a client, you can bet someone else will be, and you'll lose out.

Working longer hours than the competition isn't the solution, and spending more time chained to a desk doesn't necessarily make anyone a better illustrator either. If you can only commit to a couple of hours a day, that's fine – what's most important is following through with that commitment. Doing the work when you feel inspired is easy; showing up on the days when you don't feel like it – and giving it your best effort anyway – leads to an exceptional career. (We'll be looking at how to create and sustain your creative habit in Chapter 5.)

You get out what you put in

How every individual approaches their career and craft will be different, but being a great illustrator is a choice: one that needs to be made repeatedly until it becomes second nature. As we've seen, committing to the work and striving for continual improvement is what sets a great illustrator apart from the competition – but it's easier said than done.

At every stage of your career as an illustrator, you'll have the option to stop developing and settle into something comfortable (which many will choose), or to continue on. Most people don't: when they start getting good reactions to their work, they continue making it at the same level – after all, if it ain't broke, don't fix it!

But *great* illustrators stretch beyond that comfort zone: when they carry on developing their skills they rise above the competition, and their value increases in line with their skill and experience.

The illustrators with the most successful careers get there by having the right attitude and dedication to their craft. And as mentioned previously, they keep going, even when they don't feel like it. They're motivated to achieve great things, and they accept that it takes time to get there.

There are plenty of people who would like to be illustrators but won't ever get past it being a hobby – if they're not putting in the practice, showing their work to potential clients or treating it like a job, that's all it will ever be. This is the hard stuff which we'll return to throughout this book. An illustrator who chooses to master their craft and all the skills that go along with it, earns the title.

Everything you achieve as an illustrator will be the direct result of your own skill and hard work. You're in the driver's seat: you decide when to work, what to work on and who to work for; also, how hard you work, and how you present yourself and your illustrations to the world.

It's true that there's a lot about the freelance world you can't control – but the way you show up and the decisions you make are totally up to you. Every project you win, every fee you negotiate and every satisfied client are all down to your effort.

The more you put in, the more you'll get out of it.

Expand your skill set

Again, it goes without saying that becoming a professional doesn't happen by accident! If you've studied illustration at university, you've had time to experiment and explore the creative part of the job, which is great – but of course, practice, training and development all continue after your degree.

To have a long and successful career, continuous professional development will be an essential part of your daily practice. It's important to keep current with trends, technology and techniques to stay relevant in the creative part of the job. Many other skills are worth developing that play an equally important role in turning your creative skills into a business (we'll look at communication, negotiation, professionalism and more later in this book).

The good news is that we live in a time where we can choose our mentors, learn from some of the world's best creatives and thinkers, and tap into an abundance of resources online – that's all great education, and for very little money.

Picking up lots of useful information from other illustrators by following their careers is a great way to go: many share their knowledge through podcasts, videos, online courses and blogs. You can find valuable lessons in their mistakes and avoid making the same ones. Several online learning platforms also offer incredible classes in everything from basic drawing techniques to 3D animation (we'll look closer at online training and professional development in Chapter 5).

A freelance career is a business, so developing good financial habits and negotiating skills, along with gaining an understanding of the legal matters relevant to your career, are all important for success. (We'll be looking at these in depth, from Chapter 10 on managing your money through to Chapter 14 on licensing, rights and contracts.)

Above all, don't forget to keep reading (there are some excellent books for you listed in the Further resources section at the end of this book). Be sure to read about running a small business, sales, marketing, productivity and creativity. Investing in professional development is never a waste of time, but it's also true that reading books alone doesn't make us an expert; it's important to put ourselves out there, face down those fears and learn from experience too. (I've read a lot of books, but I've discovered plenty more from trying things out, making mistakes and trying again!)

In the next chapter, we'll look at some of the common challenges you might encounter as you take your first steps into freelance illustration.

Key takeaways

- Keep a beginner's mindset throughout your career.
- Make the most of being a beginner.
- Becoming exceptional requires consistent effort.
- Illustrators who continue to learn and improve can rise above the competition.
- Invest in your creative professional development and other complementary skills.

2

Facing challenges and overcoming barriers

Do you feel like an impostor?

Feeling like an impostor is a natural part of being human: when we share our creative work with the world, we're exposing something personal – something we've invested time and energy into and care deeply about. We have no way of knowing how the industry will react to our work, once we put it out there.

It's completely normal to doubt ourselves and feel out of our depth at times, or find ourselves wondering if a client will discover we don't know what we're doing! The truth is, everybody experiences this to a degree: whether they're a new artist, parent or president. People with decades of experience from all walks of life have moments of self-doubt – everyone is winging it to some extent and making it up as they go along.

What's also true is that at some point in their past, the most experienced and confident creatives had to choose to put their insecurities aside and show the world what they'd been working on behind closed doors – and the world is a better place because they did. Many others have never taken that risk, and kept their creative work to themselves. Who knows what musical masterpieces or great inventions we've missed out on, just because a brilliant mind didn't believe they were good enough?

Getting over impostor syndrome

The key is to focus on the progress we're making day-by-day and the increasing value we can offer to our clients, rather than letting insecurities hold us back. Don't let a voice in your head tell you you're not good enough, based on superficial things like wealth, fame or 'likes' – those metrics don't define your worth, either as an illustrator or a person.

If we compare ourselves with other, more experienced illustrators, we might find it easier not to compete than to risk failing. It's too easy to put things off which can help us improve, such as showing our work to clients or people in the industry who can offer helpful feedback.

You might not be able to conquer impostor syndrome entirely, but you can certainly take it one step at a time by practising showing your work and skills, and celebrating small achievements (to help with this, we'll be looking at some quick wins in Chapter 5). If you put off showing your portfolio until it's 'finished' – which might be several months of work – understandably, there will be a lot of pressure for it to be a success.

But what if you were to share each illustration as you complete it, or something you're happy with from your day's work every day? Sure, you might get some lukewarm reactions – but you'll also find encouragement and enthusiasm.

Sharing small achievements as you go can build up your confidence: it helps you get used to different reactions and how to respond to them. You'll get used to receiving feedback, and won't feel as much pressure for each piece to be well received – plus those reactions can inform and improve the next piece you make.

The confidence conundrum

Confidence certainly helps when you're showing your work and trying to win projects, but it's often the case that the act of doing those things is how your confidence actually grows. This is a tricky puzzle because you have to be confident in your work to win those projects, but you only gain confidence by winning projects.

The visual arts often attract introverts who sometimes shy away from uncomfortable situations. You might well feel like this while developing new skills, such as communicating with clients, responding to feedback or promoting yourself – and it's really only by pushing through that discomfort that you'll come to feel more at ease doing them.

But faking confidence can help.

Fake it till you make it

Faking confidence can work to an extent. From the early days of self-help literature, acting as if we're confident has had a history of being able to get us through that initial discomfort. Believing that we can succeed in something gives a genuine boost to our motivation and confidence.

Modern sources such as the 'Charisma on Command' YouTube channel[3] analyse footage of famous confident people, breaking down their learned or innate personality traits into actionable tips, such as:

- Being able to laugh at yourself
- Improving your body language by smiling more and being relaxed
- Improving your posture
- Making eye contact
- Dressing to impress
- Speaking more slowly and intentionally.

---

3   Charisma on Command (2020) 'How to be confident', YouTube playlist. Available at: https://www.youtube.com/playlist?list=PLefV978fp07fd4nkr1Wwfvjgz3rgtCQ8W

Acting as if you're confident could get you better results, which then starts to feed back into your real confidence; but it doesn't necessarily address the root cause of low confidence.

If you're a beginner and don't feel confident in your abilities yet, you're probably seeing yourself accurately because you have an appropriate level of confidence based on your current skill and experience. It would be unusual for an inexperienced illustrator to feel completely sure of their work. It's fine to be comfortable with your present degree of skill, and okay with what you haven't achieved yet.

Impostor syndrome can fill us with self-doubt and lead us to tell ourselves that we're not good enough – but recognising and accepting limitations is an excellent place to start. From this baseline, we can begin to identify our strengths and advantages.

The most successful creatives tend to share certain values and attitudes: they believe in their abilities while also being realistic about their shortcomings. They're optimistic, ambitious and persistent, even when they haven't had a job for weeks.

If you can see yourself clearly, you'll know what you need to work on; then it's only a matter of time until you develop the skills you need to move forward.

There's another side to confidence, which is overestimating our abilities. This is less common in creative types, but a little bit of knowledge in a subject can easily lead to overconfidence. A person might confuse doing something a lot with actually getting good at it.

It's not always easy to see ourselves and our abilities accurately, but regular self-reflection and getting feedback from others are all helpful (we'll dive deeper into this in Chapter 7).

Fear of rejection

There's a long list of fears that a new freelancer might face:

- Speaking to clients
- Negotiating
- Making mistakes
- Not being paid fairly
- Not being able to find any work in the first place.

These are all perfectly understandable reasons to be apprehensive.

We can't start out knowing how to handle all the problems we'll face in our careers. But as we've seen, we can also end up finding excuses not to do some of the most important tasks our job requires, simply because it's easier to avoid them.

For example:

- A client offers us slightly less money than we hoped for – so we avoid negotiating, because it's easier to charge less than we're worth than to have an uncomfortable conversation
- We avoid picking up the phone to have a difficult conversation with a client – because we can send an email at the end of the work day instead, and not have to deal with the fallout until tomorrow

– and so on.

Avoiding the hard stuff

Occasionally, I speak to new artists keen to make illustrations for their online shop, such as prints and products; often they're also interested in licensing their existing work to clients. Making a passive income as an artist is possible, but it's not easy to do as a beginner. Sometimes, an experienced artist with lots of fans and an existing client base can make this transition easily enough because people already want what they're producing.

When digging a bit deeper into these new artists' motivations for wanting to move into these areas, I've noticed a common theme: they don't have to put themselves out there and communicate directly with people who could hire or reject them.

Obviously, there are legitimate reasons for wanting to make money while we sleep, but this can also be an attempt to avoid the uncomfortable process of contacting and working with clients directly.

For some, fear is a compass. What they fear doing the most is what they know they actually need to deal with, so they acknowledge the fear but don't indulge it. They also realise that not facing these fears leads to something far worse: not moving forward. Much of the anxiety that illustrators experience can be boiled down to fear of rejection: clients can say no to working with us, or reject our price or ideas.

A lot of the feedback that illustrators receive from clients in the early stages of their career is rejection, simply because there's so much competition: just because they can supply illustration doesn't mean there's a demand for what *they individually* are making right now. There are more aspiring illustrators than projects to keep them busy, so clients can choose the best they can afford.

But as we've seen, as you become more skilled and experienced, you'll face less rejection. Exceptional illustrators have far less competition, because the others who haven't been able to get over their fears will have stopped pushing, or given up completely. (This is the same with people trying to get into elite sports, actors and screenwriters trying to find their big break in Hollywood, even doctors and lawyers. The people who commit to becoming the best in their field get the best jobs and opportunities, and illustration is no different.)

Getting comfortable with rejection means you can show your work and contact clients without fear: the more you do this, the more opportunities you'll have. No one can flip a switch and be automatically okay with rejection, but it is possible to practise – the more you confront it, the better you'll be able to handle it.

It's understandable that you might not feel ready to work with high-profile clients yet. But if you can switch mindset from 'I don't think they'll hire me, so why bother?' to 'Why not try and see what happens?', you can pitch your work to them anyway. Even if the answer is a 'No', you'll come to realise that it is just a 'No' – regardless of who the client is. The worst that can happen is actually not that bad.

If you're already working with a few clients, you might try putting your price up by 10, 20 or 50% for the next project, and see what happens. If they say 'No', so be it – but they might say 'Yes'.

Of course, rejection is a part of life – but it can also be proof that we're pushing our boundaries in a positive way. If we're never rejected, perhaps we might be too cosy in a comfort zone and not living up to our full potential as a result. It's also an chance to discover what's possible and where the *real* boundaries are, rather than the ones we might have constructed for ourselves.

Getting comfortable with rejection

If you'd like to see an extreme (and very funny) example of someone practising rejection, Jia Jiang's TED talk: 'What I learned from 100 days of rejection',[4] is a great watch – it's been viewed almost 10 million times at the time of writing.

Jia discusses the internal conflict of having big ambitions but being too afraid of rejection to try. He goes on a mission to get over his fear by intentionally seeking out rejection: from asking for a tour around a supermarket warehouse to successfully getting a Krispy Kreme store to make him a custom Olympic ring doughnut!

Jia came to realise that if he stuck around a little longer and didn't run away from rejection, he was becoming more at ease with these uncomfortable situations – and often was able to turn initial rejection into an opportunity.

Comparing your work to other illustrators

Comparing an illustration we've just completed with the work one of our favourite artists can leave us feeling a bit disappointed. After all, the early work we produce won't compare with what might be the 700th illustration that artist has created. And it's okay that we aren't quite as experienced as them yet: if they have five, 10 or even 20 years' more experience, there is no fair comparison. The quantity of pieces an illustrator makes isn't necessarily a measure of quality, but the amount of practice they've put in over the years surely is.

In the words often attributed to Mark Twain, 'Comparison is the death of joy', so don't make a habit of comparing your work to other illustrators: they all have a different story, goals, priorities, education and life experience. It's possible to learn a lot from other people's work if we analyse it, but comparing our own work to the world's best

4   Jia Jiang (n.d.) 'What I learned from 100 days of rejection', TEDxMtHood talk, TED.com. Available at: www.ted.com/talks/jia_jiang_what_i_learned_from_100_days_of_rejection?language=en

illustrators too often could find us talking ourselves out of trying to get there as well.

The only way to get to their level is by running your own race and making something only you can make.

Exercise: Part I – Analyse other illustrators' work

Instead of being in awe of what your illustration hero creates, ask yourself:

- Why have they made these creative choices?
- What could they have done differently, or not done at all?
- How would I approach the same problem?

Asking yourself these questions helps you begin to understand how a great illustrator thinks about solving problems through analysis rather than comparison.

Part II – Analyse your own work

There are only two people you can compare yourself with and gain some meaningful insight: who you were yesterday, and who you want to be tomorrow. That's the only comparison that matters!
Ask yourself:

- Is today's illustration better than the last one – and how?
- Did I give it my best effort?
- If not, why not?
- Am I working towards becoming my ideal, successful, productive, creative and valuable professional illustrator self?

Rehearse scenarios and prepare scripts

If you might be experiencing any of these challenges – fear, low confidence or feeling like an impostor – it's helpful to develop scripts for situations in which you might find yourself. You can rehearse what to do, how to act and what to say in advance of a potentially tricky situation.

We all do this to some degree – imagining how a difficult conversation might go and how we might react is a normal thought process – but if it's not planned and our mind runs away with us, it can lead to unhelpful anxiety. (I know I've dreamt up all kinds of worst-case scenarios when I've needed to speak to someone about a serious issue.)

Here are a few examples of situations you could find yourself in as a new illustrator:

- Introducing yourself to a potential client
- Applying to an agency
- Receiving difficult feedback on your work
- Being asked to work on something for a low price, or for free
- Being rejected or ignored by clients.

You can avoid acting or reacting poorly in the moment by intentionally considering how to approach these situations beforehand. (This is by no means a complete list; we'll explore more of these scenarios in Chapters 7, 8 and 9 and consider some of the different ways to respond.)

How to prepare for difficult feedback

When faced with difficult feedback, we might feel angry or upset – even see the reviewer as an enemy and not appreciate them for their help.

Preparing for the possibility of a difficult review takes the heat out of an emotional response because if the worst happens, it won't take you by surprise. You can reply with a polite and thoughtful response and thank the reviewer for their time – let them know they haven't wasted their effort talking to you.

You then become free to consider their comments as helpful direction rather than an attack.

Preparing stock email replies to different scenarios means you won't have to think too much about your response each time: you can simply tweak the script depending on the feedback you receive. Unfortunately, it's a fact that rejection and unreasonable requests will happen often in your freelance life: if they set your blood boiling each time they do, you'll waste a lot of energy being angry or upset. That time could be better spent being creative and enjoying your work.

After you've been working professionally for a while, you'll have faced all manner of questions, issues and problems, and will be much more confident responding to them. Until then, it's good just to be prepared.

Be persistent

After being rejected by an art director, many illustrators give up trying to work with that person again – they might feel deflated or embarrassed by a negative response. However, just because they've said 'No' to you right now doesn't mean they'll say the same to you forever. In another six months, you'll have more new work to show and will be more experienced. That art director will change their mind if you offer them something they want and can use.

It's possible you might not be sufficiently experienced or your style isn't refined enough yet, but you can get valuable feedback from these early introductions, if you ask for it (see Chapter 15 for more on good introductions).

Worth the wait

A brilliant illustrator I now work with submitted her work to the agency six times before her portfolio was a good fit for us. I can still see the first few emails now, and it's impressive to see how her work progressed over three years. The difference between the first introduction and the email that made the right impression is enormous.

If that artist hadn't been persistent and demonstrated her dedication and commitment, we never would have heard from her again. The agency would have lost out on working with an exceptional illustrator.

She did us a favour by keeping in touch with us.

Some artists submit their work to clients and illustration agencies like clockwork every few months, emailing the same old images. If those illustrations didn't work the first time, they're not going to work the fifth time. Offering something new and demonstrating your ability to develop and get better is essential.

Competing for work

Before the internet, illustrators needed to be close to publishers and advertising agencies, usually in cities. They had to go out and meet people to sell their work. Illustrators were hired for being convenient, responsive, easy to work with and, of course, skilled. Now the industry is global, everybody is convenient: any client can contact the best illustrators in the world and work with them – if they can afford them.

There was nowhere near as much competition back then; but as we've seen, illustration is a lot more competitive now. Every year, more illustration graduates are trying to get noticed – and because there's more supply than demand, you'll be competing with other illustrators for every project.

Suppose another illustrator gets a job you want. In that case it might be due to the client's style preference: it's simply not a good fit, and out of your control. But you can still ensure that all the other factors – communication, professionalism and presentation – are the very best they can be. Then if you don't get the project, you'll know you did everything right, you just weren't the right person for it this time. That's fine too, and you can move on with no regrets.

Again, not being chosen for projects is unfortunately a part of the job: it happens, no matter how skilled or experienced we are. The best thing to do is make a great impression on any client you come into contact with, because if you weren't right for this project, maybe you will be for the next one.

How to be lucky

Luck plays a significant role in a creative career: being seen by the right art director at the right time can have considerable impact. Lots of established illustrators have been lucky with projects and opportunities, but it wasn't entirely in their control.

The more we create illustrations and work on our skills, seek out opportunities and grow from setbacks, the luckier we're likely to be – these things are within our control. Consistent, smart work is a much better strategy than waiting around for a lucky break, or hoping the right people will find our portfolio or social media profile.

By actively seeking out those people and showing them your work, you're taking things into your own hands and purposefully steering your career.

Skill is worth more than talent

In our industry, talent isn't quite as big a factor in the success equation as people might think. It can give us a head start in the creative part of our job, but a career isn't built on talent alone; plenty of gifted artists never make any money from their work.

But skills – whether drawing, painting or marketing – can be developed by anyone willing to put in the effort. You aren't stuck with the level of natural talent you're born with, which is reassuring! There are lots of talented illustrators, but as we've already seen, a truly skilled illustrator is rare. Being labelled 'talented' suggests it comes easily or naturally; perhaps it might for some, but skills are acquired through hard work and dedication, which in turn helps you take control of the course of your career.

Don't find your passion, build it

In *So Good They Can't Ignore You*,[5] Cal Newport says that it's bad advice to follow your passion. He proposes that the 'Passion Mindset' – do what we love and hope the world will offer us a big break (which is how many creatives approach their work) – is less useful than what he calls the 'Craftsman Mindset': a focus on producing value with our work.

The craftsperson asks themselves these questions about their work:

5   Cal Newport (2016) *So Good They Can't Ignore You: Why Skills Trump Passion in the Quest for Work You Love*, Piatkus.

- Who is it serving?
- What is its purpose?
- Is it meaningful to anyone other than me?

The answers to these questions will give them a clear path. They work at something until it does its job well and provides value to others. Conversely, the Passion Mindset is self-centred – 'I make what I want and hope people want to buy it' – but the fact is, nobody owes us a career. Instead, it's earned by providing something that clients want.

The focus of an illustrator's career shouldn't be about what the world can offer them, but what they can offer the world – and if what you can give is exceptional, the opportunities are endless.

Author and marketing expert Seth Godin offers another point of view on passion in his book, *Linchpin*[6] that it's specific to people, not the projects they work on. Some people are passionate about what they do – but if that project, job or art form were to be taken away from them, they would find passion in something else.

These two ways of thinking about passion complement each other well. It's not about *finding* your passion; rather, *applying yourself passionately* to something.

Worrying about finding your true passion – and wondering if illustration is the right path – can be a time-consuming distraction. Time spent worrying and wondering is time not spent on becoming valuable to the industry or building your career. By adopting the 'craftsman mindset', your skill set will grow: you'll prove to yourself and others that your work is useful and valuable.

Having passion for our work is important, but it really comes from committing to the work. If you might be feeling unsure about the route you're on right now, that's totally normal – but it can lead to worry and anxiety. Settling on a path and finding out how to create value will ignite that passion in you.

In the next chapter, we'll look at the essentials to develop your freelance illustration career, as well as strategies to prioritise important work and stay focused.

---

6   Seth Godin (2018) *Linchpin: Are you Indispensable? How to Drive Your Career and Create a Remarkable Future*, Piatkus.

Key takeaways

- Make sure everything you can control is the best it can be, and don't worry about the things you can't.
- Learn from experienced illustrators – don't compare yourself to them.
- Recognising your limitations means you can figure out how to improve.
- Get comfortable with rejection, because it's not a judgement! It just a part of the job.
- Until you become confident in your own abilities, be prepared for different outcomes and situations.
- A client who has rejected you in the past will hire you if your work becomes something they want.
- The skills you pick up are far more important than natural talent.
- Be a craftsperson – make work that clients want and value.

3

Your start-up essentials

What's essential

To work as an illustrator, you need:

- The tools to create the work
- A selection of work that's good enough to get clients interested
- A functional website to present your work
- An email address and phone number.

With these in place you can make the work, have somewhere to display it and clients can contact you. There are a few more things that would be useful, and a whole load of things that aren't essential at all, such as:

- Designing a business card
- Printing mailouts
- Designing a logo and personal branding
- Attending networking events
- Having a custom website built
- Writing a blog
- Building a social media following.

These all have their benefits, but the right time to work on them isn't at the beginning. When you're starting out, there is a clear priority list:

1. Make a portfolio of work that's good enough to get you hired.
2. Show that work to the people who can hire you.

This might seem like oversimplifying, but our time and energy have their limits. When there are so many options around how we could spend our work time, choosing what not to do is key. We could spin

20 different plates and try to do a little bit of everything, or we could concentrate on the two tasks that will actually move us forward.

For example, if you have a day job, there won't be enough time to do everything – but there will be enough to do the most important things. Every hour is valuable, so try to fill each one with activities that enable you to take meaningful steps toward your goals (we'll explore this further in Chapter 5).

If the goal is to get paid to be an illustrator, the shorter the time it takes to go from making the first version of your portfolio to getting paying clients, the better. It's absolutely fine to leave worrying about the non-essentials until you're making an income from illustration: once you're being paid by real clients, you'll know it's worth investing in some of them. And ultimately, if you discover you can't find paid work as an illustrator – or decide to change course and do something else – you'll be glad you saved your money.

What's not essential

There are many non-essentials, but here are some hard truths which can help direct your time and money wisely:

- If nobody is looking at your website except you, redesigning it isn't an important task.
- There is no point designing and printing marketing materials, if the recipient throws them away because the work isn't up to the right standard.
- Getting your 'About Me' text perfect is a waste of time if no one will read it.
- Spending time getting our name out there by entering competitions, blogging about our process, posting on social media platforms and going to industry events isn't nearly as important as introducing our work to real clients directly.

Once you're getting regular paid work, you can share actual client projects on social media. You can also reinvest some of your earnings to upgrade your website, and get printed marketing materials made with an illustration style you know is good enough to make an impact on the clients you approach.

When you're making money from illustration, you're a professional illustrator. That's the best time to start investing in those non-essential but nice-to-have things, safe in the knowledge that you're on the right path.

Better kit doesn't make a better illustrator

When it comes to creating your illustrations, naturally you know what you need to get the job done! But the good news is that you don't need the newest, most expensive equipment to be a great illustrator. The difference between the latest tech and a three-year-old model is minimal, but the price tag definitely isn't – so before spending a fortune on new gear, ask yourself if it will actually make you a better illustrator. (We'll look some more at money matters in Chapter 11.)

If your tech is causing you more headaches than it's worth then sure, it's time for an upgrade. Otherwise, don't waste your money; instead, master the equipment you have available. Good kit doesn't make a good illustrator: the end product is what's important rather than the tools you use.

If you use traditional methods for your illustrations, you need to be able to scan or photograph the work to a professional standard, but that doesn't necessarily mean having to buy your own scanner or camera. You might be able to borrow them, or ask someone else to do it for you when you've got a batch of new work. If you can't, buying second-hand kit works just as well.

If you can find ways to save money without sacrificing quality, just go ahead and do it. Don't allow shiny new gadgets to distract you from what's important: making great work and getting it in front of the right people.

Prioritise your time

Finding the time to work on a new career can be difficult – there are only so many hours in a day, after all! But if you really want to become an illustrator, finding a way to carve out the time to work on that is going to be vital.

We all divide up our time throughout the day differently, based on our priorities and default activities. For some, priorities such as work commitments, exercise or spending quality time with a partner, family or friends are rightly non-negotiable. But when we're not spending time on these, we have default activities that we switch to almost unconsciously – and some are more productive than others.

For example, some might choose to read a great book or working out as their default activities, which is admirable and positive: for me, it's streaming movies and TV, while for others it could be gaming, hanging out with friends or, dare I say it, scrolling through social media! Some of these are healthier than others of course – and recreation is important – but I certainly wouldn't consider streaming TV a priority: it can take up a lot of my time if I don't actively prioritise something else.

If you can't find the space to work on your portfolio or acquire new creative skills, the truth may be that it's simply not a priority for you right now, and that's okay. But it's important to realise that without making your new career your primary focus, it might never happen.

This kind of sacrifice might mean cutting down at the start on other activities you enjoy, such as socialising or hobbies – but you also might be able to find time by reducing some less productive default activities. (A whole evening binge-watching a TV series can take a big chunk out of my day, and there's an awful lot I could do with that time if I cut down too!)

Shifting our mindset and prioritising any habit or activity that's worth doing is a positive step forward: it turns that conscious choice into the thing we want to do more than anything else. It could be exercise, meditation, cooking nourishing food, saving money, having a healthy sleep pattern or whatever might be traditionally considered good habits – all of these require us to say no to something else.

It really comes back to commitment: wanting to be an illustrator badly enough means making it a priority. There will always be other things to distract us or convenient excuses not to do it – and of course, every new illustrator will have different demands on their time and other things they want and need to do. We simply can't do everything at once: someone with 100 goals is about as likely to make meaningful progress on them as if they have none at all.

But by choosing to prioritise just one thing and focusing on that, we can achieve an awful lot.

Exercise: How much time can you commit?

Try the following steps to work this out.

1. Make it a project of paying attention to how you spend your time: identify your usual daily tasks and track how long they take.
2. Figure out how much time you can put into illustration each day.
3. Then, start small and build up. For example, if you can give an hour a day for three weeks, try 90 minutes for the next three, and two hours for the weeks after that.

It's only when you've identified exactly how much time you're spending on different things that you can see opportunities to move things around, or do less of the least productive activities.

Naturally, we all need rest and leisure time, so working out your available space needs to be realistic and manageable enough to stick to in the long term. Once you've established what you can cut down or out, you're freed up to use that new-found time wisely.

Finally, don't try to do too much, too soon – once you discover what a manageable and sustainable work session is for you, you'll be able to keep to it for longer.

Protect your time

As we've seen, if we only have a few hours to give to illustration each week, using that time effectively is crucial to focus on those high-value, essential activities we've discussed – as well as allowing ourselves quality time free from interruptions.

Often, being deliberate about structuring our work time is overlooked, but it can make a big difference to our productivity. One of the benefits of being freelance is choosing our own hours: for example, we might be at our most creative and productive in the morning (a 'lark'), or do our best work at night (an 'owl'), or perhaps somewhere in-between the two.

If we make conscious choices around when to start work each day, do creative work, take breaks and tackle other, less cognitively demanding tasks such as admin and checking email, we can stay in control of our time.

Just experiment with this to find out what works best for you.

How I get into a creative headspace

I need long periods of uninterrupted focus to achieve this, so I remove distractions and try not to multitask. I hide my phone and turn off email.

For me, a quality hour of work is 1 x 60 minutes, not 6 x 10 minutes. I can't get anything meaningful done if I'm interrupted at random intervals.

I've tried out a lot of productivity techniques over the years, and the one I return to often is the Pomodoro Technique.[7]

The Pomodoro Technique

This involves setting a timer for 25 minutes and focusing intently on the work you're doing without distraction. Then, taking a five-minute break and repeating as necessary. It's simple and effective – 25 minutes is a manageable amount of time to concentrate.

Note that the five-minute break isn't an interruption, it's a planned rest and reset – so it's key not to look at your phone or check email during that time. Rather, step away from any screen and take a beat.

You can stay in control by using this technique and make meaningful progress on a project. And because you aren't distracted by notifications, you can get into the right frame of mind.

It's possible to do this for an hour or five hours, depending on the project. It's easy because all your breaks are built into the system.

---

7   Francesco Cirillo (2023) 'The Pomodoro Technique'. Available at: https://francescocirillo.com/products/the-pomodoro-technique

Turn off notifications

In a world of push notifications and instant messaging applications such as WhatsApp and Slack, technology has trained people to expect immediate results. We Google questions and get immediate answers; we send an email or text and expect the other person to respond quickly because they have their phone nearby, all the time. There are many advantages to being so connected, but it's rarely conducive to focused work.

Illustrators don't need to be glued to their inbox. Notifications can be switched off – we can choose when to look at new email, which might only need to be a couple of times a day. Meanwhile, the rest of our time can be spent getting into the flow of creative work.

By not making a conscious decision to check emails at specific times throughout the day, we could be refreshing our inbox several times an hour. If we're checking our email or phone that often, that's just as many interruptions to our concentration.

There is a cost to switching between tasks. Research from the University of California[8] found that it takes on average 23 minutes for focus to return to a task after interruption. Interestingly, the interrupted work was performed faster, but out of necessity – people who are inter-

---

8   Gloria Mark, Daniela Gudith and Ulrich Klocke (2008) 'The cost of interrupted work: More speed and stress', *Proceedings of the SIGCHI Conference on Human Factors in Computing Systems*, April: 107–110. Available at: www.ics.uci.edu/~gmark/chi08-mark.pdf

rupted experience more stress, frustration and time pressure. Rushing is far from ideal, especially for creatives – we need to get into a creative headspace to do our best work.

While multitasking[9] might make us feel more productive, it actually makes the quality of our work worse and we end up getting less done. An hour that's unfocused and broken up by distractions isn't the best use of that time – what could easily have taken just one hour might end up taking two or three, if we regularly switch our attention to other tasks.

Social media is a distraction

Social media can be a valuable tool for professional freelancers, but it also can be a major time thief for new artists. The difference between 700 and 1,000 followers is unimportant (and it's hard for an artist who hasn't developed their skills to even get close to that amount anyway).

Your following will come naturally as a by-product of working with great clients on exciting projects, rather than the other way around. The key is aiming to be the kind of artist people want to follow: a professional at the top of their game. It's much easier to win fans when you're producing exceptional work for the best clients in the world.

Social media is designed to distract you: those platforms want you to be on there as much as possible – and it goes without saying that if you're busy doing that, you won't have time for the essentials! By all means use social media as a tool to share your work, but just be sure to schedule it and stay in control.

If you want to share something once a day, log in one time – then log out. If you keep going back to check how your post is doing seven or eight times after that, not only will it eat into your time, it'll negatively impact your ability to focus. Looking at stats can quickly become an unhealthy obsession: the jump between 50 or 75 'likes' on a post doesn't make a bit of difference to your career!

9   Paul Atchley (2010) 'You can't multitask, so stop trying', *Harvard Business Review*, 21 December. Available at: https://hbr.org/2010/12/you-cant-multi-task-so-stop-tr

Stick to a schedule

We've mentioned this briefly already but to be consistent, create a schedule you can stick to long-term:

- Decide which days and times you'll work
- Define them
- Be specific.

It's important to decide all of this once and commit to it, because having to make those decisions every single day means you'll be inconsistent: you'll only work when you feel like it and your progress will be slower. Having decided once means you don't need to think about it again – you won't need to leave it up to your future self to choose whether to show up!

You'll feel more inspired to work once you get started, and your mood will lead your actions. As we've seen, a creative who chooses to work even when they don't feel like it reinforces to themselves and others that they're a professional who gets the job done, no matter what.

Here's another thing to consider. If you don't make these decisions and communicate them to the people around you, those people will control your schedule. They won't know not to interrupt you unless you ask them not to do so.

If you work from home, talk to the people you live with about how much uninterrupted time you can have. Or if you text or speak on the phone with friends or family often, you might need to alert them of your plan to 'go dark' so they don't worry. If you communicate to them why you need that time, they'll understand – and they'll do their best to help you protect it.

How to set yourself up for a good day's work

If you struggle to sit down and get on with work, here are some ideas to make it easier and more enjoyable.

Curate your workspace

It's a good idea to keep your workspace tidy, organised and nice to be in. 'Tidy' can mean different things to different people; but either way, you can easily make your workspace somewhere you like to be!

Try creating an appealing environment with, for example, your favourite art on the walls, plants on the desk or furniture and accessories you like. If you do this, you're much more likely to want to spend time there.

Hide your phone

If your phone interrupts your work, keep it away from your desk. Occasionally, people need to be quickly contactable, but for many of us that's an illusion. As mentioned earlier, we've been trained to think we need to be immediately available for other people's demands – but for every interruption that's a genuinely important message, there are many more unimportant ones. For the ones that are important, even most of those don't require an instant response – whether the sender thinks it does or not.

Eliminate on-screen distraction

This could be as simple as making sure your computer desktop is tidy. Or it could be as extreme as blocking your computer from accessing the internet or other specific, time-sucking interruptions for a fixed amount of time, using focusing apps such as Freedom.[10]

Pick up where you left off

At the end of his writing day, Ernest Hemingway would leave a sentence half-finished: when he sat down to work the next morning, he didn't have to think about what was next. He simply continued the thought and got straight back into the flow of work. Try this technique with your work, and see how you get on.

---

10   Freedom app and website blocker: https://freedom.to (available on IOS, Android, Mac and Windows).

Time block to organise your day

Try planning your day the night before with this handy method, so you can hit the ground running in the morning.[11]

Say it's a Tuesday, and you have an important task to do the next day:

1. Consider how long it will take you.
2. Add another 50%, just in case you run into any complications.
3. Sketch out a quick timetable on Tuesday evening that shows that block of uninterrupted time you need to spend on the task on Wednesday.
4. If you feel uneasy about being uncontactable for a couple of hours, add a 15-minute email block at each side of it.

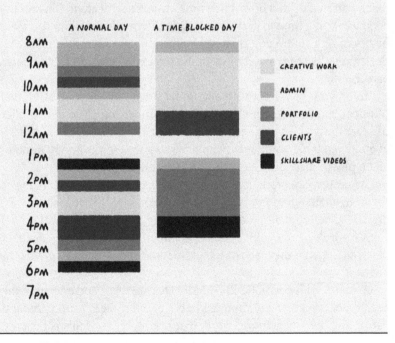

---

11   Time blocking has been around for a long time, but it's been popularised more recently by productivity writer Cal Newport in *Deep Work*. Cal Newport (2016) *Deep Work: Rules for Focused Success in a Distracted World*, Piatkus.

You'd be surprised at just how little you're missed when you try this. Most people won't notice you're gone – but you'll definitely notice the difference in how much you can do in a day, when you allow yourself the space to concentrate on a task without interruption or switching tasks too often.

Less wasted time and distraction means you'll be able to do a good day's work inside a reasonable number of hours. If you're working a 12-hour day, there's no way you can be productive and creative for that whole time – so aim for deep, focused work for a few hours instead. Cut out the non-essential tasks and limit your time to increase effectiveness.

The solution isn't working more hours, it's working smarter.

Get to work

Once you've decided how much time you can dedicate to illustration each week, it's time to get to work. Whether that's a desk in the spare bedroom or a studio you share with other creatives, you've made the decision to be there to get on with the job and make progress in your career.

To do your best creative work, do be sure to allow yourself some physical, mental and emotional space. If you're too close to reminders of other daily tasks that need to be done, it'll be hard to focus. Working at a kitchen table with other people passing through every 20 minutes and a pile of dirty dishes in the sink is far from ideal!

Wherever you work, make it the place you associate with being focused, challenging yourself and being creative. If it becomes a drop-in zone for chatting or procrastinating, changing that won't be easy. As we've seen, taking breaks is important – as is being sociable – but your actual workspace needs protecting so that you can get the most out of it.

A studio with energetic illustrators sharing ideas and encouraging each other is a great environment to be in, but if there's more disruption happening than meaningful work, that is a problem. If this is the case, make it clear to your studio mates why you're there, as a respectful work environment is important. If they can't acknowledge that, it might not be the right studio for you.

Too many unproductive days in a row will wear away at your motivation, and you'll have nothing to show for your time. But a day of focused work where you make meaningful progress toward your goals will motivate you to do it again and again.

Short-term pain for long-term gain

As we've seen in this chapter, the non-essentials are easy and low risk: it's tempting to get wrapped up in tasks that make us feel productive, but don't actually advance our career. We can keep ourselves busy for months working on unimportant tasks and still not have a paying client at the end of it.

We've also seen that it's the essential ones that count. Creating the best work you can and showing it to potential clients may be the most difficult parts of your illustration career – but they're also the best possible uses of your time.

The time between beginning and finding those first clients should be repetitive: illustrate something, show it to some clients, then illustrate some more. As gruelling as this might seem, one day you'll land your first real client, then another and another – and that's exciting. You'll find it was worth all the effort!

In the next chapter we'll look at how to develop a great illustration portfolio.

Key takeaways

- Focus on what's essential and save the non-essentials until later.
- Master the equipment you have available to you.
- However small the amount of time you can commit to illustration, stick to it and build on it.
- Reduce interruptions and distractions.
- Protect your workspace and work time.
- The most challenging things to do are usually the most important.

4

Developing your portfolio

Your portfolio doesn't need to be perfect

As we saw in Chapter 2, your portfolio doesn't need to be perfect to attract paying clients, just good enough. It's important not to wait for your portfolio to be 'finished' before you start sending it to potential clients, as it won't ever be so – it's an ongoing process of evolution and improvement. In fact, the first version of your portfolio won't be immaculate – it might not even be terribly good – but you'll learn a lot from the act of producing it, and will be able to improve it for versions 2, 3 and even 23.

Good enough will turn into great, once you're making work for clients regularly. Besides, if you're constantly improving, perfect is impossible! We can never reach our full potential, but that's actually not such a bad thing: the more we improve and grow, the more potential we have. After all, if you're going in the right direction, the best piece in your portfolio now might soon be something you take out as your skills develop.

What to include

A good portfolio is planned and developed strategically, so every part of it does a job and nothing is there that doesn't need to be.

When putting your portfolio together, ask yourself:

- What do I need to show? It's key to include appropriate work for the sector or industry you want to serve. For example, if it's packaging or branding, you'll need to have examples of illustrations suitable for those areas.

- How many examples does the client need to see? They need enough to know you're competent in what they're looking for, but they don't need to see 20 examples of very similar projects.

Every illustration that goes into your portfolio should serve a purpose. Here are a few examples:

- Illustrating a subject you haven't tackled before – so you can attract clients from a new field
- Showing off a particular skill – such as drawing, composition or narrative
- Presenting a specific format – such as a book cover or event poster
- Showing examples of work you've done for real clients – paid commissions
- Working in the style of a particular brand – so you can pitch to that brand.

Even if an illustration is just decorative, think about how it will be useful to you and, more importantly, to clients. For example, every part of a car is designed and planned – not every part has a technically necessary function, but the design and decorative elements do serve a purpose.

Why are you including it?

Before working on a new illustration to add to your portfolio, try this exercise. It'll help you focus, prioritise and make work that advances you.

It won't always be possible to answer all these questions straightaway – it's good to play and experiment, this is essential for an artist – but asking them might help to improve what you're making.

Exercise: Add value to your portfolio

Ask yourself:

Why am I making it?

- Was it a deliberate choice, or am I making it on a whim?
- Did somebody tell me to make it?
- Is it part of my strategy?
- Does it fill a gap in my portfolio, or is it something I'm comfortable with because I've done it before?

What problem does it solve?

- Does this illustration communicate an idea, or help to tell a story?
- What does it do?
- What is its purpose?
- Is it useful?

What am I learning?

- New skills, new efficiencies, nothing?
- Am I pushing myself?

Is it valuable to a client?

- Would they pay for it?
- What could they use it for?
- Am I showing them how they could use it, by mocking it up into a particular format?

Is this the best use of my time?

- Will it help me get more work?
- Will it add something new to my portfolio?

Your portfolio jigsaw puzzle

Try viewing your portfolio like a jigsaw: identify the missing pieces and think about what would fill the gaps to complete the puzzle.

Subjects

Here are some questions to guide you:

- What subjects are illustrated a lot in magazines or adverts – what's trending?
- What kinds of subjects are frequently illustrated rather than photographed?
- What subjects do illustration agencies list on their websites?

An art director might not consider you for their project if you don't have examples of popular subjects in your portfolio. Given a choice between an illustrator with examples of the subject they're looking for and one without, they'll usually go for the one who shows they can do it.

Skills

What skills are you showing in your portfolio?

Aside from your style and the medium you use, a client wants to see what you can do with them. Demonstrating your technical skills is important, but things like composition and communicating a complex idea, or telling a story with an illustration, are just as important.

For example, if you're good at painting watercolour landscapes and that's the only thing you show, it's all you're ever likely to be hired for. If you could turn your skills to, say, botanical watercolours or paintings of food and drink, you'll be able to work with different kinds of clients.

Displaying a variety of skills opens up greater scope for other projects and opportunities.

Formats

If you want to illustrate book covers, take some time to research what they look like for different genres, add illustrations that could work to your portfolio and try out some typography. You could try out several kinds to practise this skill and broaden your appeal to publishers, for example:

- Thrillers/crime
- Science fiction
- Romance
- Popular science
- Smart thinking
- Business
- Fantasy
- History

– and more.

If advertising or packaging is your goal, show illustrations that fit those formats, for example:

- Billboards
- Posters
- Gift boxes
- Labels
- Wrapping paper.

This means making up your own projects. Don't rely on a client using their imagination to see that your style is a good fit for their project.

It's not that they can't imagine it, they just don't need to – some other illustrator will be showing them examples of exactly the kind of work they want.

If you want to work with a specific kind of client, it's vital to show them you can do what they need – so to solve your portfolio puzzle, follow these steps:

- Choose the subjects you want to include or skills you want to demonstrate
- Consider the kinds of clients you want to attract
- Focus on making something to the best of your ability for each of those areas.

By the time you've completed all of these, you'll have a more well-rounded portfolio that shows different kinds of clients how they could use your work.

Who are your illustrations for?

Commercial illustration often has broad appeal, but the best work also targets a well-defined niche. Advertising campaigns aren't aimed at everybody, books aren't aimed at everybody, and your illustration portfolio isn't aimed at everybody, so thinking about who the work is for is crucial in making work that people want.

Just to be clear, this work isn't for your social media following – they aren't going to hire you. It's great if they do like the work you make for clients, but an artist making work specifically to please their online followers isn't a commercial illustrator; they're a different kind of artist.

The work isn't for you either – of course you want to enjoy the work you make, it'll be better if you do! – but a commercial illustrator makes work that's useful for clients.

If you can find the overlap between what you love to make and what people will pay for, you've struck gold: you're providing something valuable *and* having fun doing it. A professional artist's success is measured in part by how many clients want to pay for their work – that's the 'commercial' bit.

Exercise: Identify your clients

Ask yourself these questions about the three categories of people who will see your work. Cast your mind forward to these future scenarios:

The client (whom you may be working with right now)

- What is the client's goal with this project?
- What's their brand?
- Are they trendy and exciting, or formal and professional?
- Are they local or global?

The customer (your client's client)

- Who are they?
- What do they like?
- How old are they?
- What do they dislike?
- What excites them?

Your potential client (people who could hire you in the future)

- Can a potential client browse for something specific and find what they're looking for on your website?
- Is there anything to interest art directors from different fields? The list is endless, but here are some examples:

  - Scientific journal
  - Food blog
  - Children's publisher
  - Cosmetics brand
  - Technology company
  - Airline.

Anyone and everyone in the world is not a potential client. It's key to define your niche, because trying to please everyone means your work can only ever be average. The most famous artists, musicians and writers aren't creating for everybody, and creative work that tries to please everyone is just background noise – safe, bland and unmemorable.

There will be people who don't like your work – maybe even a majority – but it's not for them. As long as you've defined your target audience and they like it enough to pay for it, you can make a career out of it.

What do your illustrations do?

Illustrators are problem-solvers. We use our skills to make images for different purposes, but the common theme is that they all have a purpose and job to do. If our illustrations don't provide a solution for a client, they don't really need them – even if they look good.

Exercise: What job is your illustration doing?

When you're working on a new illustration, ask yourself these questions:

- Could it attract a particular type of consumer to a product?
- How does it make a customer feel about a brand or a product?
- Does it make someone feel good about themselves?
- Why do I like it?
- Does it tell a story?
- Is it instructional?
- Does it communicate the client's values?
- Does it attract attention?
- Does it help to explain an idea?
- Does it inspire?
- Is it light-hearted or serious?
- Does it solve a problem?

Whatever the answers to these questions are, dig deeper:

- How does it grab someone's attention?
- Whose attention is it grabbing?
- What makes it serious?
- Why would the illustration appeal to one kind of customer and not another?
- Does the illustration do what it's supposed to do?

If it does, it's good. If it doesn't, figure out what you can do to make the next one better.

Curate your portfolio

As we touched on earlier, your portfolio website serves two essential functions: it shows your work and gives potential clients a way to contact you – everything else is secondary.

It's important that your portfolio doesn't function as a place to store everything, or as an archive of every piece you've ever made. Instead, it needs to be a selection of your best work – a curated gallery designed to attract paying clients.

In 'How to Take Smart Notes', writer and researcher Sönke Ahrens describes an archive as a 'bin for the indecisive'.[12] If you were to put every piece of art that a gallery can access into a single space, you'd have a warehouse – not an exhibition!

How many images should you include?

Twenty to 30 images is plenty, but there is no magic number for how many should be in your portfolio. A portfolio with 10 images won't show enough of your skills or include a broad enough range of subjects, but one with 50 could use some editing. The work you leave out has just as big an effect as the work you include.

---

12   Sönke Ahrens (2022) 'How to take smart notes: One simple technique to boost writing, learning and thinking', *The Zettelkasten*. Available at: https://www.soenkeahrens.de/en/takesmartnotes

I'm often asked how many images should be included in a portfolio, usually by new illustrators who don't have much work and are trying to assess how long it will take for their portfolio to be ready to show.

For example, a client who wants to hire us to illustrate patterns for packaging needs to see enough examples to trust that we can complete the task to a professional standard – four or five may be enough – but not so many that our portfolio doesn't show any variety. The difference between, say, including five and 10 floral patterns is minimal.

Too much of the same subject creates diminishing returns: the more you create, the less valuable it becomes to you – and the less interesting it is to a potential client.

It's possible you might not have enough work to fill up a portfolio page right now, so doing that will be a priority. However, showing work we're not happy with or that's less than our best effort, just for the sake of getting those images in, doesn't serve us in the long run either. It's fine to take your time.

Because developing a portfolio involves making new work consistently for as long as it takes to get it good enough for clients to hire us, it means making more good illustrations – and often bad ones, too. A common mental block for creatives is thinking that everything they make *has* to be good. If they feel like they can't make something good that day, they don't make *anything* – and this stops them from improving.

Don't let the fear of making bad illustrations hold you back, because those are the ones from which you'll learn the most. Your portfolio will be constantly updated with your best work *so far* – so the more you make, good or bad, the better.

How to tell a joke... and refine your portfolio

I challenged myself to try out stand-up comedy for a short time just for fun, and had the pleasure of seeing and being on stage with some hilarious acts.

A stand-up comedian on tour might deliver the same set 100 times around the country, and the timing and the delivery are perfect every time. But before that tour starts, they'll have told every joke in the set with different timing, intonation and phrasing around the stand-up circuit, night after night. The painstaking practice, when a comedian tries a joke out for the first time to half-hearted titters or complete silence, never crosses most fans' minds – they only see the finished product.

The only way that first idea becomes a great joke is by exposing it to feedback from lots of different audiences, then the comedian's ability to refine and deliver it perfectly. They do that with every line in their show, and you'll do that with every illustration in your portfolio.

Most of your fans and clients will only ever see your best work. They won't consider the years of practice it's taken to develop your skills.

Creating a great portfolio is a career-long process of refining new additions and editing the parts that aren't working any more – much in the same way that not every joke makes it to the final show.

How to identify a commercial style

A commercial style is simply something a client can make use of and is happy to pay for: it appeals to them and their customers, and can help them achieve their goals as a business.

When we're inexperienced as illustrators, it can be difficult to know if our style is commercially viable – but with a bit of research, we can find out what works and why. If you look through magazines or illustrated products in shops and supermarkets, you can see lots of different commercial illustration styles.

Exercise: Part I – Research other illustrations

Next time you're out and about, try this simple exercise with the illustrations you come across. Look at the styles these illustrators are working in, and what kind of clients are hiring them.

- What are their features?
- How are they made, or what techniques have been used?
- What makes them suitable for the brand?
- Why do you think the client liked this style?

Make a few notes on what you observe and what you don't, and see if any patterns emerge. Do your illustrations fit into these patterns? Analysing what makes a successful illustrator's style popular gives you useful information.

- Is it the colours they use?
- Is it the mood they convey or the bold statements they make?
- Do they draw characters in a particular way or illustrate clever conceptual ideas?
- What is it that you personally like about their work? If you're part of their target audience, that matters.
- Look at illustration agencies and see what kinds of artists they represent. What styles are good clients paying for on a regular basis?

Ask what your friends or family like about particular styles, as you might be surprised at the insights you gather. If they all like a particular style, it's likely to be commercially viable – clients will pay for that.

Part II – Analyse your own illustrations

Next, take a hard look at your own style.

- Does it have the potential to be on a book cover or advert?
- Who are the customers or readers that would buy a product based on this style?

- Are they young or old, professionals or students, rich or poor, mainstream or alternative, and so on?

For example, a style that appeals to a niche of young, poor, alternative students isn't going to pay as well as a style that appeals to mainstream wealthy professionals.

If an artist works in an unusual or weird style – if it's chaotic and unrefined, or the subjects are grotesque and explicit – they're limiting the kinds of clients that will want to (or can) hire them. There might be one or two decent jobs for the styles that are 'out there', but struggling between occasional projects is a lot less appealing than being in demand by a variety of clients. Commercial illustration makes money.

Why unique illustration styles sell

As well as being commercially viable, a freelance illustrator's style should be unique to them. If we work in a style that's just like fifty other illustrators', not only are we competing with all those experienced artists, we're not going to be memorable either.

Agents want to work with illustrators with a strong, personal and consistent style that clients remember. Brands want to work with illustrators who can offer something that leaves a lasting impression and helps them stand out from their competitors.

Plenty of jobs are available for an illustrator who works in a generic style or multiple styles, but rarely are those illustrators chosen specifically – they're hired for projects that require *any* competent illustrator. It is possible to make a decent living being a convenient, well-balanced and competent all-rounder – but you'll never be able to command the highest fees or work on the most exciting projects. If your work looks the same as those fifty other illustrators, the client will simply choose the cheapest option. As we've seen, the most interesting clients want the most interesting creatives – and are willing to pay the highest fees to work with them.

- Do you want to be generic or unique?
- Do you want to be hired because the client needs *any* illustrator, or do you want clients to know who you are?

You might already follow some of the world's most unique illustrators, know their names and remember their styles. These artists make a strong impression and clients ask for them by name. They may even write briefs specifically for them.

You won't appeal to everyone by being unique, but the people and clients who do like your style will be real fans. They'll hang it on their walls and try to hire you whenever they can, recommend you to others and pay you well for your work. A unique artist contributes something original to the world, rather than simply going with the flow and following trends.

Make a name for yourself. Be unforgettable!

Next, we'll look at the creative habit and how to build momentum in your career.

Key takeaways

- A portfolio only has to be good enough to get clients interested.
- Show samples of the kinds of work you want to do in your portfolio.
- The goal of your portfolio isn't to please everyone.
- Illustrations have a job to do.
- Think of your portfolio as an exhibition of your best work, rather than an archive.
- Unique illustration styles are memorable.
- Aim your work at an audience that can pay you.

5

Forming and maintaining your creative habit

You have to start to be great

There will always be reasons not to start or commit to the path you want to take. Perhaps you might be telling yourself you need to take a few more classes, or save up a bit more money before you go for it? Or maybe you've been working on your portfolio for six months, but haven't taken that all-important step of reaching out to potential clients.

The best time to start was months ago, but the next best option is to start today.

As we saw in Chapter 2, one major reason why people don't take the plunge is fear of not being good enough. You don't have to be a great illustrator to start, but you do have to start to become a great illustrator.

Celebrate your mistakes

You might not succeed on your first try, but if something is worth doing at all, it's worth doing badly until you can do it well. No one can think their way from being a beginner to an expert! Instead, they try, fail, learn, reiterate and improve. Evolution works by trial and error and as we've seen, the hundredth illustration we produce will be much closer to being great than the first.

Common mistakes

Here are a few common mistakes to look out for – no doubt they were frustrating for those artists in the moment, but their experience can help you to avoid them yourself:

- Agreeing to work on a project that you know you're not well suited for, or won't enjoy.
- Not saving work regularly, losing hours of effort and missing a deadline as a result.
- Not reading a brief carefully and producing work to the wrong specifications.
- Sending blanket emails to multiple clients – and being called out on it!
- Spending hours figuring out how to do something in Photoshop, then discovering a button that does it automatically.
- Applying to an agency and typing in the wrong name.

Of course, these things happen at times – and they can be so embarrassing if someone notices! But being unprepared to make at least some mistakes means not getting out of our comfort zone long enough to create anything original. If an illustration doesn't work out how we wanted it to, there's still something to aim for and we can still learn from it. If we give up trying after a setback, we have nowhere to go and no way to improve.

Turn mistakes around

You can use mistakes to figure out what pieces of the puzzle still need to be added to your skill set, then go practise them. Own up to mistakes, learn from them and apologise: admitting we might be wrong doesn't make us appear any less competent – it's actually a display of honesty that people respect. If an artist doesn't have a few failures or plenty of mistakes under their belt, they can't really consider themselves an expert. They've missed out on too many opportunities to develop their skills and mindset.

When you can appreciate that mistakes and setbacks are essential for progress, you can begin to celebrate them. You can be glad you've done something wrong, because you'll be one step closer to doing it right next time.

Your first clients are for motivation

Getting your first paying client is an incredibly powerful motivator. When a client recognises and values your work enough to pay for it, you have proof that you're doing something worthwhile.

As we saw in Chapter 3, focusing on the essentials and tackling the difficult tasks are priorities, because it minimises the gap between starting your creative career and generating an income from it. Being distracted by non-essentials is a common trap for many illustrators which can lead to loss of motivation, even quitting altogether.

Regardless of who those first clients are, they will be a primary source of motivation to keep going – they're the evidence that you've got what it takes and that this is a legitimate career path for you. Of course you'll aspire to working with big-name clients, but don't let that take away from your early successes. There will be plenty of time for those bigger and better clients in your future.

Small steps in the right direction

Naturally, you don't need me to tell you that successful and long-lasting careers aren't built overnight! They're the result of consistent, incremental improvements and small steps in the right direction – and your portfolio will grow steadily, one piece at a time. You might produce a lot of work quickly at the start, but you'll build a truly exceptional portfolio over a longer period. The occasional sprint is good for us, but our career is the long-term goal.

Every day we dedicate to our craft is worth celebrating, because what begins as a small, manageable daily work session becomes more than the sum of its parts over time. Having a regular routine of working on our illustrations reinforces commitment to our craft: with each passing day, our motivation grows and our skills and portfolio get better. Just like physical exercise, consistency is key for strengthening your creative muscles – as we've seen, it's better to work a little and often rather than attempting long creative sessions intermittently.

This is known as 'compounding': rather than taking big strides and leaps toward a goal, it's more about small steps in the right direction, sustained and uninterrupted for a long time. If you're inconsistent in how you work, you might find yourself taking one step forward and two steps back. But if you can practise your skills for just an hour a day and focus on small, incremental improvements, your progress compounds into enormous development over time.

Exercise: Make tomorrow better than today

If you have an off day, it's easy to improve the day after.

But let's imagine you have the best, most productive and creative day: what's one small thing you can do to make tomorrow even better, capitalise on that momentum and do more of what's already working?

For example, could you:

- Find a small efficiency in your workflow?
- Introduce yourself to one more potential client?
- Set aside time to practise a skill that you know will help you?
- Make progress on a project you've been putting off?
- Focus on a task for 30 minutes instead of 25?

Whatever it is, plan it out at the end of today and commit to trying it out tomorrow. Even if you do it badly, keep at it each day and try and improve on the day before. With every improvement, no matter how tiny, even 1% movement raises your baseline of quality, effort and achievement.

Do this every day for a month, year or five years, and you'll be a completely different illustrator!

It's also fine to accept that not every day will be an improvement on the last, despite our best efforts. Some days will be more challenging than others, but what matters is the intention to keep improving. We experience success less like a straight line and more like a squiggly one filled with good and bad days, plateaus, setbacks and opportunities. As long as you keep coming back day after day, the trend will move in the right direction.

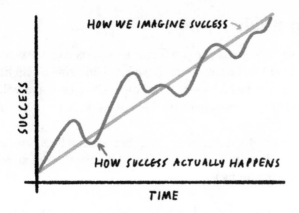

The Flywheel Effect

In his book *Good to Great*,[13] Jim Collins introduces the 'Flywheel Effect'.[14] He describes a large, heavy wheel that a business must push round and keep momentum going, even if progress seems slow or non-existent at times.

The key is to be consistent in pushing in the same direction. Over time the effect kicks in, and the wheel spins faster and faster with the same amount of effort. No one rotation is more important than another; it's the combined effort of pushing in a single direction consistently that drives the flywheel to spin increasingly quickly.

For an illustrator, the Flywheel Effect means consistently creating new work, building a solid portfolio and refining skills. Each new project, contact and skill you acquire is a turn of the flywheel, building momentum and bringing you closer to your goal.

Keep pushing, creating and improving, so the Flywheel Effect can work in your favour.

13   Jim Collins (2001) *Good to Great: Why Some Companies Make the Leap... and Others Don't*, Random House.

14   Jim Collins (2023) 'The Flywheel Effect'. Available at: www.jimcollins.com/concepts/the-flywheel.html

Setting goals

By setting specific goals, we can focus our efforts and work towards something tangible. For example, if we know the kind of clients we want to work with (which we touched on in Chapter 4, and will expand on in Chapter 8), we can create the kind of work that will be valuable to them.

Without a set of specific goals, both big and small, our efforts can be scattered and ineffective. We can only hit what we aim at, otherwise we're just relying on luck – throwing things at the wall and seeing what sticks.

Having clear purpose in doing the work can help us to avoid distraction and stay motivated: this sense of purpose drives us forward, even during challenging times, and gives us a reason to keep pushing towards our goals.

A goal is only good if it makes us take action in the present: if it excites and motivates us, we're more likely to follow through with it.

Try to set goals which are aspirational and slightly above your current skill level, but not so difficult that they seem impossible. If they're too easy, you won't push yourself to improve; but if they're too ambitious, you might become discouraged before coming close to achieving them. Give yourself a specific timeframe to complete your goals, too. They can be short-term or long-term, but do give yourself a date to aim for.

Exercise: Set some goals

What's most important for you to achieve in the next three, six or 12 months? Here are a few ideas to get you started:

- Make a list of clients you want to work with, and find out what they like.
- Work on different subjects to make your portfolio more well-rounded.
- Publish your portfolio online by a specific date.
- Study a new skill or technique.
- Stick to a work routine for 90 days.
- Get in touch with an industry professional for feedback.
- Secure your first paying client within three months.

Remember, goals are just a motivational tool – don't beat yourself up if you don't hit every one! The intention to aim at something will help you stay focused, but you might find you decide to abandon a goal as time goes on, or perhaps you'll realise it was a bit too much right now and save it for later. These goals – whatever they may be – aren't about getting perfect results, they're simply about getting better. It's fine to reassess and throw them out if you need to do so. Don't let them become a source of anxiety.

Intermediate goals

For example, if we're straight out of college and our goal is to work on an international advertising campaign within the next six months, we might be setting ourselves up for disappointment. As we've just seen, it's important to find a balance between aspiration and achievability – so setting intermediate goals you can realistically celebrate along the way will keep you motivated.

In this scenario, your intermediate goals could look like this:

1. Develop a bold, eye-catching style suitable for advertising.
2. Get feedback on your work from an advertising professional.

3. Apply that style to a range of mocked-up adverts to add to your portfolio.
4. Introduce your portfolio to 20 advertising art directors, producers or buyers.

You can see from this list that a collection of goals becomes a more concrete plan of action. It's a long project, so you can break down the steps and celebrate as you tick each one off.

On completing your short-term goals, you could add new ones which are slightly beyond your immediate grasp, so you'll always be looking to improve. As well as shorter-term goals, you could keep the international advertising campaign or whatever else you choose as a longer-term, aspirational goal.

If you ever feel lost or approaching burn-out, be sure to take notice of that as it's a message just to stop and regroup. Consider different ways to approach your long-term goal and if needs be, adjust your shorter-term goals to give you some more attainable steps to celebrate along the way.

Planning your next steps

While setting goals can give us a sense of direction and purpose, trying to plan out our whole career when we're beginning is simply impossible. There are too many variables and factors we have no control over:

- Opportunities can come up leading to unexpected results
- The market and economy might shift in unforeseen ways
- Personal priorities can change over time – what we want in five years may well be different from what we want now.

It's also important to say that visualising and setting goals isn't progress in itself. We shouldn't spend so much time imagining and tinkering with our goals that we don't actually get around to doing the work!

Be sure to review your goals every few months to stay on course, but stay in the present too and focus on what you can achieve today. Rather than fixating on long-term planning, focusing on the short term can be far more effective.

You can't predict the distant future, but you can probably predict what your working day will be like tomorrow with a decent degree of accuracy! Concentrate on making the small units of your time – the hours and days – the best they can be, and the months and years will take care of themselves.

Quick wins

Motivation can be elusive: it comes and goes, especially at the start of our career when we're not being hired yet. Obviously, the faster we can get real clients, the better – nothing beats the validation of someone wanting to pay for our work – but we can't control how long that will take. In the meantime, what we can do is look for opportunities to celebrate milestones and find quick wins, as this helps us stay motivated.

Here are some ideas to get you started.

Competitions

These can be a useful way of giving you a project to focus on – doing well in a competition encourages you to continue. Not everybody can win, but just entering and sharing your work is an accomplishment in itself, and a good excuse to add a great new piece to your portfolio.

Study

Try taking an online class to improve a skill. Many of us have unfinished courses we've signed up for and neglected (more on this below). If I'm having a low-energy day, watching an online class is a good way to get my creative engine into gear. I often feel inspired to try something new after doing this.

However, choose your resources carefully: high-quality input = high-quality output.

Share your work

You can do this with five, two or even just one potential client. Try asking for some feedback or a portfolio review from somebody in the industry too.

Explore others' creative work

Find out about other people's creative success via books, blogs or podcasts. They don't have to be illustrators to inspire you (see the Further resources for some examples to check out).

Challenge yourself

If you challenge yourself to complete, say, 10 illustrations this week, ask yourself:

- How would I need to plan my time differently?
- What will I have to sacrifice to make that possible?
- What non-essentials will I have to cut?

Celebrate ticking off challenging items on your to-do list, adding new work to your portfolio and every step you make that gets you closer to your goal. As we saw earlier, social media can be a useful tool if used mindfully, but it can easily fool us into feeling productive. Contacting one real client to show your work could be worth fifty social media posts.

Online learning platforms

When it comes to getting an education in illustration, access to the internet means there is no barrier or shortage of great options for top-quality courses in all kinds of technical and creative subjects – not to mention all the other associated skills we might need to do the job.

Some incredible instructors make classes for online learning platforms, such as CreativeLive, Skillshare, Domestika and Udemy (see the Further resources). We can find out anything we want online for a fraction of the cost of traditional institutional education.

The trouble with online courses

Unfortunately, completion rates for classes on these platforms are also terrible. For example:

- Udemy reports that the average user only completes 30% of a course they've purchased.
- The completion rate for online courses ranges between 5% and 15%.
- An average of 70% of users never even begin the courses they buy.[15]

What could this tell us?

- Some of the classes may not be worth completing because they're low quality.
- The barrier to entry is very low: courses might cost between £10 and £200, but these platforms have regular promotions, sales and free trials.
- Users aren't committed to finishing what they start.

The problem with online professional development is that it's too easy to quit. Quitting college or university is difficult: there's a high financial and social cost to dropping out. No one will ever know if you don't complete an online course, but if you leave formal education, everyone that you know will know about it – so that decision isn't taken lightly. And as much as online platforms might devise ways for students to interact with each other, there isn't nearly as much of a social incentive to stay as there is with further or higher education.

How to find good courses

There are plenty of low-quality online courses, but they're easy to avoid. Users rate them and the cream rises to the top, so it's not difficult to find the best ones. What if you were one of the 5 to 15% of people that regularly complete the really great online illustration courses?

15   Rokon Zaman (2020) 'Completion rate on eLearning platforms – alarming!', *The Waves*, 14 July. Available at: www.the-waves.org/2020/07/14/completion-rate-on-elearning-platforms/

You'd have a significant advantage and could level up your skills faster than most others who don't finish what they start.

This goes for reading too: a study from 2022[16] claims that more than 50% of Americans haven't read an entire book in over a year. If you can read some books on art, creativity, marketing and small business skills, you're already ahead of the pack (see the Further resources for some of my personal favourites).

Don't wait for inspiration

Inspiration has been written about by many great creative minds, including Picasso, Stephen King, Thomas Edison and my art school hero, Chuck Close. All of these well-respected creatives have discovered independently that the more creative work you do, the better you'll get –and the more inspired you'll feel.

Like passion, we've seen that inspiration is discovered by doing the work, practising and always coming back to do more. The more you do it, the more often inspiration will strike.

If you've decided you can work on your illustrations for say, 20 hours a week, be sure to stick to that plan, whether you feel inspired or not. As creative professionals, if we have to wait to feel inspired before getting to work, we'd rarely produce anything good – or even at all! It's true that inspiration will come and go, but it will show up a lot more frequently if you're at your desk.

In the next chapter, we'll be looking at practising your craft and why it's meant to be challenging. If you're ready for that, see you there!

16   Nicholas Rizzo (2022) 'Over 50% of Americans haven't read a book in the past year', *Words-Rated*, 13 July. Available at: https://wordsrated.com/american-reading-habits-study

Key takeaways

- The sooner you start, the sooner you'll improve.
- Don't worry about making mistakes – they're a great way to learn.
- Consistent practice and tiny improvements will compound over time.
- Set a mix of short-term and long-term, easy and difficult goals.
- Find quick wins to keep you motivated.
- You'll feel inspired a lot more often if you practise regularly.

6

Practice makes progress

A great portfolio takes time

As we discovered in Chapter 4, a great illustration portfolio can't be made in a rush over a couple of months; instead, it's developed from habitual and regular additions, incremental improvement, editing and consistent time and effort.

Even so, the results may not reflect that – there will always be unforeseen problems to deal with and days when we're not quite as productive as others. However many illustrations we make, some will be better and more popular, while others won't be our best work. That's never going to change, but you can control your commitment to the process and come to enjoy it.

Don't break the chain

The 'Don't Break the Chain' method is usually attributed to Jerry Seinfeld giving writing advice to a young comedian.[17] When he and Larry David were writing 180 episodes of *Seinfeld*, one of the most popular and influential sitcoms of the 1990s, staying focused was crucial.

Every day that Jerry completed his goal of writing jokes or scripts, he would add a big 'X' to his calendar: by doing this, he had a strong visual representation of progress (I've used this method for years for different goals too). It's no accident that Seinfeld became the most successful comedian of his generation. As with many top

---

17   Gina Trapani (2007) 'Jerry Seinfeld's productivity secret', *Lifehacker*, 24 July. Available at: https://lifehacker.com/jerry-seinfelds-productivity-secret-281626

performers, that consistency is what set him apart from others.

The hard part comes if the chain breaks somewhere along the way, as it's all too easy to get out of routine. Life happens – so if you do have to miss a day, don't let that day turn into a week. If you have to miss a week, don't let that week turn into a month.

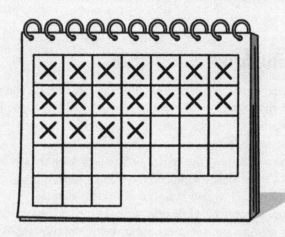

Practise deliberately

The 10,000-Hour Rule

The '10,000-Hour Rule', popularised by Malcolm Gladwell's *Outliers*,18 gives us a general indicator of how long a person should practise to become an expert. While 10,000 hours of practice in illustration certainly wouldn't hurt, this simple rule-of-thumb focuses only on the *quantity* of practice, not its *quality*.

There are different forms of practice – and they're not equally helpful. On the one hand, aimless repetition without guidance or feedback is an inefficient way to learn. On the other hand, deliberate practice involves absorbing information from great teachers, getting regular feedback on progress, working on weak points and intentionally attempting things beyond our current skill level.

Just as athletes have coaches, illustrators learn from many people throughout our careers, and should seek feedback on our work regularly. For example, an Olympic swimmer might spend hours just working on their dive or turn, while a weightlifter adds small, additional weights to improve their personal best. Illustrators can choose to deliberately practise drawing faces until we know every angle and expression. We can master new techniques, skills and technologies to inform our work and continue to evolve our style over a whole career.

As we've seen, to figure out how to do something, we need to attempt it – which expands our comfort zone in the process. For example, if you want to draw, pick up a pencil; if you want to use design software, find an online tutorial; if you're finding it challenging to generate good conceptual ideas, just come up with a list of 20 bad ones instead! Even if none of them are perfect, some will be better than others – you can discover what works for you (and what doesn't) from that process.

What general, unmethodical practice could achieve in 10,000 hours, deliberate practice can surpass in half the time. It's not about *how much* we practise, but *how effective* that practice is.

Choose the right route to success

Let's meet our two illustrator characters, Alex and Jo.

They're both starting from the same place at the same time, but are more than likely to achieve different levels of success and competence after 10,000 hours of practice.

Alex teaches himself by drawing what he enjoys, figuring out design software by experimenting, and doesn't get outside help in his creative pursuit.

Jo seeks out great instructors online, analyses other illustrators' work to find out what makes it successful, and asks professionals for their feedback.

Alex is learning by trial and error, while Jo is studying and building on what other industry professionals have already achieved – giving her a big head start.

Learning by copying

From the earliest stages of our lives, we learn by copying others. We observe and mimic the behaviours and abilities of those around us to acquire the skills we need. We learn how to cook from recipes that someone else has created, and how to exercise by watching an instructor. We study the techniques of artists we admire to improve our own illustrations.

For me, it was comic books: from the age of six to 16 I was drawing superheroes, and I can still sketch a pretty good Batman! We look, copy and learn – and that's fine, up to a point.

Adding something only you can do

When we copy to improve our skills, we draw on a multitude of resources and influences. What makes your work unique is your very own collection of influences and the additions, subtractions, changes and improvements only you can make. Copying other illustrators' work helps us develop new skills, but it can't lead to originality – not without adding something of ourselves to the mix.

For example, the ideas presented in this book have been inspired by a variety of brilliant thinkers, artists and writers who have left a lasting impression on me – along with my boss at Folio, Nick, who trained me to be an agent. Using the ideas I've been exposed to for more than a decade from books and podcasts and my day-to-day work, I've been able to build on and combine them to develop my own viewpoints on creativity, productivity, business and more into something uniquely my own. I couldn't have written this book without those influences, but nobody else could have written the same book either.

If we only copy we're never leading, only following – and we'll always be a step behind those illustrators making something new and unique. But true originality is rare: whether they're aware of it or not, a creative person is influenced by the world around them and builds on what has come before. They incorporate all their influences, then add something extra that only they can produce.

We can honour and respect the artists who have influenced us by using their work as a foundation for something new, rather than simply replicating it.

Exercise: Chart your success

Try this exercise to track your progress – and celebrate wins!

1. Decide how many hours you want to work on illustration every day.
2. Next, put up a chart on the wall – somewhere you can see it regularly – and start checking off each day you've achieved your goal.

Soon you'll be on a winning streak, and the last thing you'll want is to break the chain. It's the kind of momentum that builds enthusiasm and accountability as your focus isn't on any one day, just the process.

What happens when you reach a 100-day streak, or 200: will you break that chain?

Not if you can help it – that's powerful!

What if you're being copied?

If people are starting to copy what you're doing, that means you're doing something right: you're leading and that's something to be proud of, as frustrating as it might be at times! You can't copyright your own style, so you might encounter copycats along the way – but the illustration community does take notice of who the impersonators and originals are.

If you're concerned about someone copying your style, keeping your methods a secret won't stop them because if your work is worth copying, someone will do it anyway – whether you share your techniques or not. In fact, if you're worried about giving away your best ideas, that's all the more reason to share them. The more you share, the more you'll be recognised as an original – and as a bonus, you get to practise coming up with new and great ideas.

Because we don't find out how to be illustrators without outside influences, keeping our process a secret doesn't give us any advantages. It only adds unnecessary stress when someone inevitably figures it out.

If the creatives we admire share some of their secrets, we eagerly absorb that information and appreciate them even more. But copying a particular individual artist's work actually does more harm to the copier: they're simply reproducing work that's already complete, from which the original artist has already moved on. They might uncover their techniques, but they won't know the thought process behind the piece – and that process is what enables the artist to create more original illustrations for clients.

It's a skill that simply isn't developed by copying.

Embrace your influences

Take inspiration and absorb knowledge from as many people as possible. If your work is inspired by fifty different artists, it will look original because it *is* original. Nobody has combined those sources in the way you have before. Nobody will be able to recognise all those references. Nobody else could have made it but you.

If we only have a small pool of sources, our work will be less original and more recognisable as copies of those two or three artists. If we only copy one artist, we'll just be a poor imitation of their work; we can't do what they can do as well as them.

Honour your influences by weaving them together into something new, so your work is the result of all your favourite art styles, experiences and education. The more you experience and discover about your art, and the more you analyse creative work you enjoy, the more skills and resources you'll have at your disposal.

Productive procrastination

Procrastination is a way to put off doing the essentials: the hard stuff. It isn't a question of laziness, because (if you're anything like me) you'll know we can often put a lot of effort into tasks that delay us starting the important things!

Clearly, procrastination is an obstacle to overcome in terms of productivity, but studies have shown that moderate levels of 'putting things off' can actually lead to more creative output.[19] People who don't procrastinate and dive into their work right away might be skipping an important stage of the creative process. They latch on to the first one or two ideas they have and get to work; but someone who procrastinates for a while is leaving space for new ideas to emerge. This stage might involve engaging with a relatively easy task and while doing so, their brain is freed up to make connections and come up with ideas in the background.

Many people claim to have great ideas in the shower, when they're out jogging or even napping: these are typical examples of activities requiring low levels of mental engagement, where a problem can still be rattling around in the back of your mind. There's good reason to procrastinate if you're working on solving a creative problem; but of course that doesn't mean it should be used to avoid important work either!

Productive procrastination is purposeful: you can step away from a problem, do something else that's beneficial and still reap the benefits of letting your subconscious do its thing.

19   Adam Grant (2016) 'Six secrets to true originality', McKinsey & Company, 5 August. Available at: www.mckinsey.com/capabilities/people-and-organizational-performance/our-insights/six-se-crets-to-true-originality

Sleep on it

Salvador Dali famously had a method for generating new ideas, which involved holding a key in his hand as he took a nap. When he dropped off, the sound of the key hitting a plate that he'd placed beneath his hand would wake him up, allowing him to access his dream state.[20]

In *Steal Like an Artist*,[21] Austin Kleon recommends having multiple projects on the go at the same time, so procrastination can be productive. If you aren't making progress in one project, try procrastinating from it and switching to the other one to make progress there instead.

As we've seen, unproductive procrastination could be watching TV or scrolling through social media. The jogging example above might not be productive for your illustration work, but activities that are beneficial to your health and wellbeing, such as walking – especially in green spaces – have been shown to boost creativity.[22] There are many more examples of things that won't help you progress in your career, but can still be good for you. Choosing activities carefully, and using procrastination mindfully and in moderation, can be great ways to help your creative process.

Grow your illustration community

Often, the life of a freelancer can be solitary. Some share studios or live in creative hubs where more opportunities exist to socialise with

20   Drake Baer (2013) 'How Dali, Einstein, and Aristotle perfected the power nap', *Fast Company*, 10 December. Available at: www.fastcompany.com/3023078/how-dali-einstein-and-aristotle-perfected-the-power-nap

21   Austin Kleon (2012) *Steal Like an Artist: 10 Things Nobody Told You about Being Creative*, Workman Publishing.

22   Marily Oppezzo and Daniel L. Schwartz (2014) 'Give your ideas some legs: The positive effect of walking on creative thinking', *Journal of Experiential Psychology* 40(4): 1142–1152. Available at: www.apa.org/pubs/journals/releases/xlm-a0036577.pdf

like-minded people. Who you surround yourself with professionally is important: as discussed in Chapter 3, if you work in a studio full of creatives less committed to doing the work than you, you'll surely be influenced by their habits.

If, as the often-quoted saying goes, you are the average of the five people you spend the most time with, it's in your best interests to spend that time with people who are more motivated, committed and serious about their career choices.

Exercise: Making connections

Having a supportive community of like-minded individuals can be a significant boost to motivation and success. You can learn from them, lean on them, share ideas and benefit from each other's experiences.

Whether this is an online community or in real life, it's worth trying to make connections.

Ask yourself:

- Who can I learn from?
- Who can I connect with that can positively influence my work?
- Who can I collaborate with?
- What can I offer to the community of other illustrators?

As well as the many benefits you'll receive from your community, don't forget to give back and encourage others. Congratulate your peers on their successes and say good things about them publicly, as this builds a supportive network. Sure, you'll be competing over work occasionally, but you're all on the same journey – so why not support each other along the way?

It's also important to speak to and spend time with people who have done, or are doing, the thing you're attempting. If you're a new graduate and join a studio full of busy illustrators, you'll become a part of that professional behaviour and quickly settle into good habits. You'll naturally start to do what they do: if that means long periods of quiet, focused work, you'll get into the habit of doing the same alongside them. No doubt your colleagues will be more than happy to share their knowledge and experience with an enthusiastic young illustrator, if they see you behaving like a professional.

The next chapter is about the essential step of getting feedback. It's time to test out your work in the real world and see what people think!

Key takeaways

- A great portfolio is developed over a whole career.
- Make a chart to keep track of your productive workdays.
- Deliberate practice is more effective than aimless repetition.
- Be influenced by other creatives, then add something only you can do.
- The most challenging things to do are usually the most important.
- Turn procrastination into an idea-generating tool.
- Surround yourself with the right people.

7

Get feedback on your work

Why an outside perspective is important

While you're working on a project with a client, you'll get feedback on your progress. A good client will hire you for your expertise and unique perspective, but they'll still want to check in to make sure that what you're making aligns with their goal for the project.

There's an element of give-and-take with this process – you have your ideas, and they have theirs – but the input of a good art director can make an illustrator's work better. The roles of art director and artist are designed to work together: receiving and responding to feedback is part of the job; and as we saw in Chapter 4, this is also essential when developing your portfolio, before you've found your first clients.

When trying out styles and putting a portfolio together, as an illustrator you'll often work alone behind closed doors, trying to get it to a stage you're happy with. But often we can't see our own work objectively – we're not necessarily the best judge of our own strengths and weaknesses.

If you seek out the opinion of someone in the industry, you can get a fresh pair of eyes on your work: they can see what you can't. An outsider to your creative process doesn't see all the effort and context that affect your judgement, they only see the finished product – but this is valuable, because that viewpoint helps us see our work in the way that a client would. We can get a more objective view that isn't tangled up with an emotionally-charged creative process.

When to get feedback

Without an outside perspective on our work, we could try something out, enjoy it, feel good about the result and decide to fill our portfolio with similar work over four or five months. If our judgement of that first experiment was biased, we risk producing work that isn't viable, because the illustrations we like and feel the proudest of might not be commercially attractive. Meanwhile, the project we hated working on could be the most commercially valuable illustration in our portfolio.

We might be lucky, but it's also possible we could have spent months going in the wrong direction. Getting feedback early and often means we can discover potential problems with the work *before* we've poured too much time and energy into it. We can change course quickly and easily, if we need to do so.

Checking for bias

Let's return to our illustrator Jo for a moment, and two scenarios:

A. Jo works on a subject she enjoys, so the ideas flow freely. She discovers new tricks and skills while working on it, and things fall into place quickly and easily.
B. Jo works on a subject that's out of her comfort zone: she might even find it boring. She makes a frustrating, time-wasting mistake that requires her to backtrack and redraw a lot of it.

On the one hand, it's perfectly understandable that Jo favours her first illustration – because she enjoyed working on it. If she feels proud of that process, of course she's going to like it.

On the other hand, she might not like the second illustration as much because it was a less enjoyable process.

In both cases, Jo isn't seeing the work objectively – she is biased.

Exercise: Trial your style

Before committing to making a whole portfolio of work in a new style, try testing out some options and get quick feedback. Making 20 illustrations takes a long time, but you don't need a whole portfolio of work to ask for feedback.

1. Choose a few illustration styles you like.
2. Make two or three examples in each style.
3. Share them with other creatives, colleagues or friends and ask for their honest opinions.
4. See what kind of comments you get back, and adjust your course for the next set.
5. Repeat as needed.

If you repeat this process for a few months, at the end of it you'll have come up with a lot of ideas, developed some new skills and more importantly, be a lot more confident that your style is something the market wants to pay for.

It's been validated by multiple people, and you've refined it into its best form.

This is a great way to practise not being too precious about your work too – you may have to throw a lot out – but what remains will be your best. It takes effort to do it this way and to find people willing to offer their help; but you'll improve faster, find out what your audience responds to and have a better portfolio as a result.

Sadly, I've seen a lot of aspiring illustrators who've plugged away at the same style for years with no significant interest from clients. They're so emotionally invested in it that it's unthinkable to change course now. They might be just around the corner from a big break, but they might spend another three years not making any headway at all.

If a style isn't working, it's far better to find out quickly. You could go it alone and learn through trial and error, or develop through feedback. One way is slow and painful – but while the other may sting at times, it'll be a lot quicker.

As mentioned previously, part of the job is accepting critique and feedback. For a commissioned illustration, the client has the right to give their opinion on what we've made, if they're paying us to make it. Getting used to responding to feedback early in the portfolio development stage means being able to practise before the stakes are higher.

Your minimum viable portfolio

Software companies used to make their products behind closed doors and release them into the world, hoping for the best. Now they release a minimum viable product (MVP) for beta testing before official release.

A select number of users can try out the software, find its faults, offer feedback and help improve the product. The company can find out what's not working early and change course, if necessary. It might require small adjustments or huge, fundamental changes.

Either way, they find out early and can make improvements without unnecessary wasted time. You can use the same approach for your portfolio:

- What does your minimum viable portfolio look like?
- What's the quickest way for you to create a good enough portfolio to send to clients?
- What would you rather learn sooner than later?

Where to get feedback

It's possible to get feedback on our work from anyone, but some people will be more useful than others in helping to improve it.

Friends and family

Our loved ones might be well-meaning, but they're unlikely to be objective or experienced enough to give really good, commercial feedback. Unless they happen to be industry professionals themselves, our family's, friends' or partner's feedback on our work isn't especially valuable, because naturally they care more about making us happy than giving us the truth.

They simply might not know enough about illustration to understand how to help us.

Classmates and peers

Your peers may have limited commercial experience, if they're still figuring things out for themselves – but they'll definitely know things that you don't. They'll have different skills and interests within the subject, and can offer you at least a fresh pair of eyes. They could make suggestions that might not have occurred to you.

Teachers

Teachers are a great source of feedback, if you're still studying. Even if they don't have much commercial experience themselves, their job is to help you develop – and they're good at it. Be sure to make the most of your teachers, because you won't have access to them forever.

Professional illustrators

Other illustrators are a great option: they're already in it and making money from their work, so they must be doing something right! You don't need to go for the most famous and popular illustrators to discover something useful (more on this below).

Agents

Agents can be a good source of advice. A request for feedback might be a welcome change to all the applications they receive (more on this in Chapter 15).

Industry professionals

There are several independent professionals in the industry who can review your portfolio – usually for a fee, as they charge for their expertise.

The Association of Illustrators

The Association of Illustrators has consultants who can review your portfolio – again, for a fee.

Art directors

Art directors might be the hardest to pin down – but they're the ones you're ultimately hoping to impress, so their input will be really valuable.

Get knowledgeable feedback

The main thing is to get feedback from people who know what they are talking about. That doesn't necessarily mean going for the most experienced or successful ones in the industry either. The super-famous and popular illustrators get a lot of requests for this kind of thing, and their time is limited.

You might find it hard to get a response from professionals very high up the ladder, but you can gain a lot from someone who is just a few years ahead of you. Advice from a very experienced and successful illustrator is valuable in many ways, but it might be 10 or 15 years since they were at your current stage. Even with the best intentions, the way they got their break or found their first clients probably won't be the same way you should do it – that's if they can even remember how they did it! A newer illustrator with a few years of experience will be able to give you relevant advice that you can apply to your work, because it's fresh in their mind.

Not all advice is good advice

Having said that, not all of the advice you might get on your work will prove to be useful. Your teacher's, agent's or even my advice isn't perfect because it's our opinion – but some people's advice *is* more valuable than others.

Unfortunately, even within our industry, not everyone has developed the skill of giving constructive feedback. An overwhelmingly positive review might mean our work is perfect and we have nothing left to learn; or it could be that the reviewer is unsure about what the best course of action should be for our work. They may hold back on some of the more difficult feedback they want to give, to save our feelings.

It's not easy to deconstruct a stranger's portfolio and tell them what direction they should go in, based solely on a short meeting. People worry about steering us wrong and hurting our feelings – it's a lot easier to be positive, ignore the problems and have both parties leave the inter-action feeling good about themselves – but that doesn't help us.

The opinion of an industry professional with years of experience should be considered more carefully than that of someone who doesn't know the industry – but whatever feedback you receive, keep in mind that they are just opinions. With creative work, there is no right or wrong answer. For example, if an experienced art director tells you your style won't work, it simply might be because they've never seen it work before. They may be right or wrong – it's based on their unique experience. Ask yourself whether their experience is valuable to you.

As someone who gives a lot of general advice to illustrators online, I can tell you that there is no substitute for direct, personal feedback. There is plenty of broad advice out there to read, listen to and watch: most of it will be useful for *someone*, but it won't all be useful to *you*, as general pointers for all illustrators aren't necessarily going to be specific enough for your work.

Every artist works differently, with different goals: personalised feedback on your work is far more helpful to your development.

Exercise: Evaluating feedback

Try asking 10 industry professionals for feedback on your work, and see what comes back. You won't get 10 completely different answers: overlapping themes and trends will appear:

- If seven or more out of the 10 tell you the same thing, listen to it.
- If five people say one thing, and five say the opposite, wait and see.
- If one out of the 10 gives you a piece of advice you've never heard before, it's not a priority.

The more feedback, the better

Asking one industry professional is good, but asking 10 is better. No matter how experienced a person might be in the industry, they still have their own biases, tastes and opinions.

That one outlier may be more insightful than the other nine people you've spoken to, but they also may be giving you a personal opinion that ultimately isn't going to be useful for you.

One piece of advice from one person may or may not be helpful: you won't know if you don't try it – but that's a risky, all-or-nothing strategy. If you receive the same suggestion from a number of experienced people, it's a safe bet to prioritise that change.

Responding to feedback

When we've found people who can give us feedback, and they've made an effort to look at our work and consider it, we then have a responsibility to ourselves and them to take action.

The first thing is to thank the reviewer for their time (people tend not to be so willing to help in future if they aren't acknowledged, so it's important to extend that courtesy). Then, you have options with what to do with the feedback:

- Do exactly what the person has said, hoping they're right.
- Choose to ignore their feedback, hoping they're wrong.
- Take what you think might be useful to you and put the rest aside.

If an industry professional whose opinion we value has shared their insight and experience, we have to be willing to seriously consider their notes and try out their suggestions – even if it's not immediately obvious how it will help. If we're not open to giving it a go, their time has been wasted – and so has ours.

If we think the reviewer is wrong, we can always prove it by trying what they've suggested to see if it works. We'll never know if their feedback could have helped if we don't have a go; but digging our heels in, not taking any action and closing ourselves off to the possibility that they could be right leaves us in the same position we were right at the start – still in need of advice!

Dealing with difficult feedback

We ask for feedback because we want to improve, but it's also true that we might not like some of the feedback we get. Receiving praise can boost our motivation, but we're not getting much else out of the interaction.

Reassurance and a pat on the back doesn't help us improve or give us any clues on what to do next. For example, I don't relish the idea of receiving negative feedback on my work, but I find it far more helpful if someone can tell me what I've missed or where I'm going wrong, because I can use it to inform whatever I do next.

Nasty, unhelpful, negative comments can be safely ignored because they're not coming from a good place; but constructive, tough feedback from a trusted source can still cut like a knife. It can be hard to deal with difficult suggestions when we've worked hard and tried our best. Unfortunately, I recommend that you actively seek them out, because if you've only received good feedback on your work, you probably haven't shown it to enough people.

The parts we don't want to hear – the hard parts, the things that will take a long time to fix or need fundamental changes – may be the feedback that makes the most significant difference to our career.

Changing the small, easy and quick details isn't going to make a difference if there are larger issues to address.

How to handle negative feedback

If you receive a particularly harsh review of your work, first consider the source:

- Does the person want you to succeed?
- Do they have the experience to give weight to their comments?
- Do they have a track record of helping other illustrators?

If the answer is no, then their feedback isn't worth much. But if they're a credible source of industry experience, even though you may initially feel disheartened, they are doing you a favour.

A harsh review by someone who knows the industry well might mean you have to start your portfolio over – but as we've seen, it could save years of soul-crushing effort trying to sell your style to a market that isn't interested.

If you find yourself in this position, take a breath: get a second opinion, then focus on the next step in the right direction, however small that might be. If you decide to start your portfolio over again, instead of seeing it as a huge mountain of a task, just break it down into manageable steps and concentrate on the next action.

Start with the smallest possible improvement you can make today, and do the same tomorrow until you build up momentum again.

Don't take it personally

Once the creative process is done, it's important to practise detaching ourselves from our work. When an illustration is completed, our 'baby' has to leave our tender loving care and stand on its own two feet! It becomes its own thing, quite separate from us, the artist. It may thrive or perish, once we let it go.

Putting some emotional distance between ourselves and our work saves us from unnecessary turmoil. We aren't our work, and negative feedback on that isn't a reflection on us as a person – but it is a chance to discover something useful for the next illustration we make.

Stoically choosing not to feel upset by negative feedback is easier said than done; but we can suffer if we interpret difficult feedback as an attack. Instead, if we can see it for what it is – an attempt by someone to help us by generously sharing their professional opinion – we can be enriched rather than shaken by the experience. As we've seen, if we take critique personally over time, we'll close ourselves off to situations where we might be exposed to it. We won't be able to benefit from useful, constructive observation.

Asking for directions

If you're driving through a country village looking for a place, you could ask a local for directions. They know the area, they've probably lived there for years. If they tell you that you've taken a wrong turn, would you be offended? You might be frustrated that you've been driving in the wrong direction for a few miles, but they've given you useful information based on their knowledge and experience.

However, they can't give you good directions if you don't know where you want to go. And even if you do know, they might genuinely want to help but still give you faulty information. You won't know until you try.

Choose to trust in people's experience, even if there's a risk of it occasionally not working out.

Reflect on your own performance

What's also true is that we can be our own worst critic or biggest fan, depending on what mood we're in – still, evaluating the quality of our own work accurately is an essential skill to develop. It won't always be possible to get outside feedback, so we need to be able to see the short-comings of our work – and the areas we need to work on – to improve it.

Equally, it's important to recognise and take note of what we've done well, so we can do it again next time. While a healthy boost to our self-confidence is good, it's worth being mindful that too much can risk developing an unrealistic view of our skills.

With every project you complete, practise giving yourself a full and honest critique.

Exercise: Evaluate your work

When you've completed a project, ask yourself:

- What did I do well?
- What could I have done better?
- What mistakes did I make?
- What did I learn?
- How could I have completed this more efficiently?
- What can I improve on next time?

Some of these questions might be painful for the ego, but crucial for real development.

Seeing the flaws in other illustrators' work is easy; seeing our own is much more difficult – partly because we don't want to see them! In the same way that you might feel embarrassed about the quality of your work a year ago, try to find a way to view it with a little distance, as if you didn't create it. Detach and assess it on its merits, rather than your experience of producing it.

As we've seen, viewing our own work objectively can be hard (which is why seeking outside feedback is so essential); but practising honest self-reflection means you'll be able to see your work, with all its strengths and weaknesses, more clearly.

Here's another thing to bear in mind: while feedback is important, don't rely on external validation to keep you motivated, because it's often inconsistent and unreliable. What's more helpful is being able to say to yourself: 'The illustration I made and shared today is better than the illustration I shared last week. That means I'm getting better.' Then, move on to the next one.

Exercise: Boost your mindset

Not every day can be full of productive and meaningful work, but when there have been too many so-so days in a row, it helps to spend five minutes evaluating your mindset towards whatever you're working on.

This short exercise helps you identify any barriers to doing your best work. Being mindful and deliberate about mindset helps you improve the next day's work and get back on track.

Here are some questions to think about:

* Did I approach my work with enthusiasm and positivity?
* Was it a real grind to get anything done?
* Why – what were the reasons?
* Could I do anything differently?
* If I'm not enjoying a task, how can I make it more fun or challenging?

In their fantastic book *Make Time*,[23] Jake Knapp and John Zeratsky recommend finding a daily highlight[24] to produce a satisfying and productive day of work.

When run-of-the-mill tasks are a grind and goals seem too far into the future, choosing a daily highlight to focus on can keep us moving forward.

These highlights are split into three categories:

* What's urgent?
* What will be most satisfying?
* What will bring me joy?

---

23   Jake Knapp and John Zeratsky (2018) *Make Time: How to Focus on What Matters Every Day*, Bantam Press.

24   Jake Knapp and John Zeratsky (2023) 'Choose a highlight to make time every day', excerpt from *Make Time*. Available at: https://maketime.blog/article/choose-a-highlight-to-make-time-every-day

What's urgent?

What do you absolutely have to get done today?

Whether it's a client deadline, submitting your taxes or replying to that email you've been putting off for just a bit too long, if you have something you need to do today, make it your primary goal. If that's the only thing you do today, at least you know it's been a worthwhile task.

What will be most satisfying?

Rather than doing something you need to do, this highlight is about what you actually want to do and gives you a sense of accomplishment at the end of the day. For example, it could be learning a new skill to use in your practice, or finishing an illustration you've been tinkering with and putting it up on your website.

These are the projects you've been meaning to get around to but haven't quite found the time for yet.

What will bring me joy?

Even if the task isn't urgent or won't directly contribute to advancing your career, you might be able to snap yourself out of an unproductive rut by having some fun.

Perhaps it could be experimenting with a new technique or chatting about illustration with another creative; it might even be something that isn't related to your work but allows you space to take a breath, escape the daily grind and come back to your practice with more energy and enthusiasm. This highlight is really about being intentional in choosing a task that invigorates and brings you joy.

It's certainly true that not every day can be perfect or productive. You'll work for a lot of great clients over the course of your career, but plenty of bad and boring ones too. As we've seen, there's a lot you can't control – but you can control how you approach each workday.

Try to be satisfied with a good day's work instead of being disappointed with things you have no control over. Do your best, even if the client doesn't do theirs. Even if you spend the day just doing paperwork, a good day when you've given your best effort is something to be proud of – so celebrate those small wins.

The next chapter is what we've been waiting for: getting out there and finding some paying clients!

Key takeaways

- Outside feedback helps us see our work more objectively.
- Get feedback from lots of people, and pay attention to recurring comments rather than individual ones.
- Be willing to try out suggestions from professionals, even if it isn't obvious how they will help.
- Practise detaching yourself from your creations. Feedback on an illustration isn't judgement on you as a person!
- Regularly reflect on what you've done well and what you could improve.
- Find a highlight for your day.

8

How to find clients

Prospecting for new clients never stops

Prospecting is the process of finding and contacting new clients: it's the unglamorous, repetitive and absolutely essential part of the job, putting yourself out there and showing real clients what you can offer. There's no way of knowing how long it might take to land your first job – so the earlier you can start this process, the better.

Prospecting never stops: it's a regular process that freelancers keep up throughout their careers. They plan ahead so they have a steady flow of work, or as steady as possible – even the most popular artists have quiet periods. If we're busy with projects it's easy to let this slide, but it's crucial not to wait until all our projects come to an end before we start looking for more work.

Make this task a part of your usual workdays and do a little bit, often. It's better to do it regularly than let it build up into a looming mountain of a task you dread doing every month – because the bigger it seems, the more stressful it will be. Not only because spending three days in a row sending pitch emails is boring, but because inevitably there will be some rejections. If you do some every day, you can spread out those emotional blows and it won't be a job you dread, just a part of your routine.

Who is your client?

Part of the fear of getting in touch with clients in the early days is that we don't really know who we're contacting. We imagine an unforgiving, severe gatekeeper passing judgement on each illustration submission: those people do exist, but they're probably not the right person to contact.

Sending your work to the creative department of a company – the designers, creatives and art directors – means you're emailing people who aren't so different from yourself. They're creative and keen to have that creativity recognised by others; they'll be mostly informal at work, and they probably like illustration!

Depending on their experience level, age and type of organisation, those similarities will still vary. Even so, a 40-year-old magazine art director has plenty in common with a new illustrator: they'll remember what it's like trying to get their first creative gigs, and many of them will get a lot of pleasure from helping a new artist find their feet in the form of advice, feedback or even commissioning you.

It's worth bearing in mind that most of the time, the person you're emailing would love to help but is snowed under with other projects: they aren't an obstacle to overcome or a barrier to your entering the industry. The problem a lot of clients have is simply lack of time to do all the things they'd like to do, such as supporting others, pursuing their own creative projects or getting out of the office on time. As much as they might enjoy it, your request for work or advice will probably be low on their priority list.

However, if they work in the creative industry, they do likely enjoy looking at new work – so if you're concerned about annoying an art director with your cold emails, just assume they would like to help you if they can and that your well-considered, occasional contact is a positive for them rather than a nuisance.

It's easier to represent yourself and your work authentically if you approach this first contact with confidence, openness and good humour. If your work is good and your email is friendly and polite, you're doing this art director a favour by sending them something they can potentially make use of some day, when the right project comes along.

Give yourself a pat on the back for being so generous and helpful!

Finding and researching clients

Working for magazines is a core part of many freelance illustrators' careers. If you look up 'List of magazines by circulation' on

Wikipedia,[25] you'll find a rundown of more than 500 titles from around the world, which doesn't even scratch the surface. Not to mention all the other sectors that hire illustrators:

- Advertising
- Publishing
- Corporate
- Start-ups
- Packaging
- Websites
- Products
- Games
- Apps
- Food and drink

– and many more.

There are more potential clients in the world than we could ever hope to work for in our career. Of course, not every magazine, company or advertising campaign will use illustration, but there are plenty out there to keep a skilled illustrator busy.

Finding the art directors of those 500 magazines and introducing them to your work could be a great start, but a lot of them don't hire illustrators. Front-loading your research and finding out which magazines *do* work with illustrators saves a lot of time. It just takes a few minutes of online searching to discover whether a magazine is worth introducing yourself to, and you can narrow down a longlist into a shortlist of validated prospects quite quickly.

Research clients online

Try an online image search for '[Magazine name] illustration'. If they work with illustrators, you'll find examples from their online articles and probably links from other illustrators who have worked with the magazine.

25   Wikipedia (n.d.) 'List of magazines by circulation'. Available at: https://en.wikipedia.org/wiki/List_of_magazines_by_circulation

Don't waste time on clients that don't use illustration

I tried this myself with the UK's no. 53 magazine, *The Economist*, and Germany's no. 3 magazine: *Metallzeitung* (which, remarkably, appears to be for metalworkers and not as I previously thought, a heavy metal music magazine!).

The Economist search yields pages full of illustrations in different styles, whereas *Metallzeitung* is largely page layouts of text and photos.

I mention these ranking numbers only to show that a magazine's size isn't necessarily a factor in whether it works with illustrators. One of these is a good prospect and worth introducing your work to, while the other probably isn't.

Check out illustrators online

Take a good look at the illustrators you follow online – whose work is in a similar realm to yours – and look at who they've worked for. There will be plenty of recognisable names, but also many clients you've never heard of: make a note of them and look them up. You'll know they hire illustrators because they already have – and if they've hired one who has worked in a similar style to you in the past, they'll use *your* kind of illustration.

Build up a client list

Finding clients online takes some time, but it's not difficult work: by making it a part of your daily or weekly schedule, you can regularly add to your list of prospects. At the start of your career, before you have a client list, a reputation and followers, finding clients to send your work to is a numbers game.

We've seen and understood earlier that this stage isn't about finding the best, most recognisable clients: even with the right style and skills, it's a highly competitive market for new entrants and difficult to land big-name clients. Instead, finding any clients who are willing to hire us

– and getting paid to practise our skills and work on our portfolio until we're experienced enough to take on bigger and better clients – is the way to go.

Be open to all opportunities

At this point, be prepared to cast a wide net to find those first paying clients and open to any and all opportunities – with illustration, you never know where a project might lead. Finding work becomes easier as our careers progress, and once the hard work of researching a healthy list of validated clients is done, it only needs maintenance and updates: we can send out emails with new work whenever we choose. As time goes by, your portfolio will get better, as will your reputation – when it does, clients will start seeking you out.

Many new illustrators have a particular vision of the kinds of projects they want to work on: children's books, for example. While there's nothing wrong with having that goal, it's a long-term one. Naturally it takes time to build our dream job, so a beginner usually doesn't have that kind of choice.

Remaining open to other possibilities means any kind of project is on the table; so for now, just work on whatever you can get. Once you're too busy to say 'Yes' to everything, that's the time to choose which projects suit you best and begin steering your career in the direction you want to go. The interesting thing is that you might find that the direction you ultimately choose isn't what you originally set out to do. If you can experience lots of different kinds of projects early on, you'll have a much better idea of what you like or dislike – and what you're really good at.

In Chapter 4, we looked at developing our portfolio strategically to go after the clients we want, whether publishers, advertisers or whatever interests us. But while we're still trying to get our first clients and gain experience in the industry, our strategy will be different.

It takes time to establish yourself in a particular niche, so until then a portfolio with broader appeal can help you find your first clients. They might not be your ideal ones, but you can gain valuable experience in different parts of the industry – and perhaps even discover an area you enjoy that you hadn't previously considered.

Find those contact details

Once you've got your shortlist, all that's left is finding the name and contact details of the right person in the organisation: typically, an art director or designer.

Searching on LinkedIn makes finding the names and job roles of these people easy enough, but finding their email address can be trickier. Many are listed on the client's website, but others will be hidden and require some detective work or guesswork on your part. If you can't find the email address of the person you're looking for, perhaps you can locate the address of someone else who works for the organisation to see how they structure these, for example:

a.name@client.com
First.last@client.com
firstlast@client.com
firstname@client.com

There are common patterns in how company email addresses are formatted, and working out the person's possible email this way can work surprisingly well. Even if you can't find any email addresses for the company to give you a clue, there's nothing to stop you guessing the format of the email address. After all, if you were to try the four formats above and only one is correct, the recipient wouldn't ever know about the other three attempts.

Phoning a company can be nerve-racking for some, but calling a magazine's general enquiries number to ask for the art director's email address (whose name you've already discovered in your research) can work. If they ask why you want it, you can tell them you're an illustrator: art directors work with illustrators – what could be more normal than that?

However, contacting potential clients on social media can be a bit of a gamble: some are receptive to it, while others don't want intrusion into their personal profiles – it could risk irritating them to be bombarded with requests for work outside of their professional lives. LinkedIn is designed to connect people on professional terms; while a request to connect with a potential client, combined with an introductory email, is a much stronger foundation for a professional relationship. An art director might still ignore the email but at least it's unlikely to irritate them, being an expected part of their professional role.

Follow up on your introductory emails

If the client is on holiday, off sick or simply having a busy week, responding to illustrators won't be anywhere near the top of their priority list once they get back to their normal work routine. Your first email may get buried in their inbox.

There's no harm in checking

If you were to receive an email from someone and you didn't respond, would you think it was strange or rude for them to follow up in a few days, just to check if you'd received it? I wouldn't; it's a very normal thing to do.

If you've emailed your work to a prospect and haven't received a response, you might figure that they aren't interested and move on. But following up with a potential client who hasn't responded isn't breaking any social conventions – it's simply checking to see if they received your first email.

By sending a polite follow-up, you could double your chances of getting a response; of course, they might still choose not to reply, but you haven't been pushy or rude by sending another message. If they don't respond after the second email, move on: maybe they're not interested right now, but they might be when you get in touch again in a few months (more on this shortly).

However, should the client ignore your first email, they might be feeling guilty about it for a few seconds (especially if you asked them a question); if they ignore your second email, they may feel like they're being impolite. After all, you've generously shared your creative work because you think it will be useful to them; this could encourage them to send you a reply.

Still, even if it is a rejection, you've gained something from the interaction. Perhaps it wasn't the answer you wanted, but a sign that you still have some work to do before you can collaborate with that client. It's better to know upfront than to be wondering.

If you can double your chances of getting a reply by sending a follow-up, it's fine to go ahead and do it.

Why clients don't respond

Unfortunately, it's a fact that we don't always get responses to a lot of introductory emails, which can be quite demotivating. It's all too easy to assume that lack of a reply means those people don't like our work: that is possible, but it's also just one of a long list of reasons why they haven't got back to us.

They might:

- Think our work has potential but isn't good enough yet
- Feel our work isn't relevant for them right now
- Be away
- Be too busy to respond
- Hate our work with the fire of a thousand suns!

– or they might like it a lot, bookmark it for later but not bother to respond. There's really no way of knowing why they haven't replied. The important thing is not to assume the worst or feel too embarrassed to ever try emailing that person again.

Continuing to show our work to these clients at regular intervals may or may not lead to a paid project – but if we never contact them again, it definitely won't. It's highly unlikely that a client actually hates our work: either it's right for them, or it isn't. And if it's not right for them now, who's to say it won't be in a few months?

Give the client a reason to respond

I send and receive a lot of emails. Too many, in fact – so if I get an email that doesn't require a response, I don't respond.

When illustrators email to introduce their work to the agency, I look at all of them – but not all of them ask a question requiring a response. If there's a short paragraph about the artist and a selection of illustrations attached, the intention is clear: but there's nothing for me to reply to specifically.

If you pose a particular question – whether it's asking for some feedback, something about the brand or for an opportunity to work together – you give the client a reason to reply. There's no guarantee it will work, but it could increase your chances of getting a reply.

How to handle unpleasant responses

In the unlikely event that you do encounter someone rude to you or unpleasant to deal with, the chances are it's not your fault. They might be having a bad day or be frustrated with other things and decide, for whatever reason, to take it out on you.

There is absolutely no good excuse for someone to be angry or impolite to you after you've kindly offered your creative work to them. If this does happen, try not to take it personally. It could be an isolated incident due to various factors, or it could be a red flag that this person is neither nice nor good at their job.

Personally, I like to give people the benefit of the doubt – but I'd be unlikely to contact someone like this again. Behaving this way means the person – and the company they represent – will lose out, not you.

Keep in touch with clients long-term

As we've seen, some clients – especially the big names – want to work with the best talent; however, those clients and many others are also willing to pay for convenience and peace of mind. If we're showing up in their inboxes with great new work every few months, we'll be on their mind when the right project comes along. And if they become familiar with our work because we're reliable and enthusiastic, it won't feel like a risk to hire us.

When you only get a few seconds of attention in someone's inbox, it's hard to make a memorable impression. Be sure to keep in touch regularly, so the client gets to know your name and your work – think long-term.

Once you've landed a client and helped them solve a problem or complete a project, check in with them every so often afterwards too. If you did a good job, clients who have worked with you already will be much more likely to commission you again, because you've built up some trust with them (more on this below).

How often should you email clients?

I've spoken to illustrators who email their client list once a month, and others who do it once a year. The former is far too frequent, enough to risk irritating them; while the latter isn't frequent enough – it's important not to leave it so long that the client forgets who you are. Reaching out every three-to-six months is the sweet spot to show new work and remind them you're still there.

I've also been added to a lot of illustrators' mailing lists and newsletters. This is definitely annoying and should be avoided. By all means ask permission to add someone to your mailing list, but it shouldn't be done without consent.

Since implementation of the General Data Protection Regulations (GDPR) in the UK in 2018, it's illegal to add someone to a mailing list unless they've expressly given permission. Be sure to check the mailing rules in your country to ensure you stay the right side of the law.

Build trust with clients

We've seen previously that the first email we send to a potential client might be ignored, but that's not the important one. It's actually the fourth, fifth or eighth – the email when the client recognises our name in their inbox, we've become familiar to them and our work is finally right enough to get their attention.

Naturally, it takes a lot of patience to keep trying to catch someone's eye if they're consistently ignoring us: that's why most illustrators don't do it. They try once or twice, then give up; however, this is the sales part of your job. Every three-to-six months when you get in touch with the client, you'll have something better to share with them; eventually, it'll be good enough for them to hire you. It might take years of persistence and patience with some, but hopefully less than that with others.

Advertisers build up familiarity and interest in a product by showing consumers their adverts multiple times: maybe you'll see it in a magazine first; then on a poster and in your social media feed. Eventually, some of the target audience will become interested and familiar enough to click on the link, look up the product or even buy it.

If a client sees our work once and never sees it again, they aren't going to go out searching for us; it didn't make an impression the first and only time we contacted them – but maybe it will the fifth time. After a year-and-a-half of regular check-ins, the client could see that our work has developed and perhaps they'll have exactly the right project for our style at that time. The thing is, we'll never know if we don't keep in touch on a regular basis to build up that familiarity and trust.

It's easy to find clients and send them some work; it's easy enough to get people to follow us on social media or visit our website, if our work is good – but it takes trust for a potential client to go ahead and hire. They need to see that an illustrator can produce consistently good work, and that we can help them solve a problem. They don't want to feel like working with us is an experiment: it's why getting those first clients is by far the hardest part – no one wants to go first, because it's a risk. But the more clients you get, the easier it is to find new ones because you're building proof that you can do a good job.

In the next chapter, we'll be looking at the process of working with clients and building a great professional relationship.

Key takeaways

- Do a little bit of prospecting regularly and often.
- Assume your potential clients have the best of intentions and would like to help you.
- If a client doesn't respond, it doesn't necessarily mean they don't like your work.
- Ask a potential client a question, so they have a reason to reply.
- Front-load your client research, and don't waste time on clients that don't hire illustrators.
- If you can't find a client's email address, try guessing it.
- Always follow up after your first email.
- Show potential clients new work every few months, whether they reply or not.
- Be patient. Your first email to a client is unlikely to be the one that gets you hired.

9

Working with clients

Solve problems, don't create them

Clients need a professional who communicates clearly, succinctly and honestly – so once we start working with them, it's crucial not to put ourselves on their 'problem list'. If we add to their problems, they'll be less inclined to work with us again.

That's not to say you shouldn't include them in the creative process: they have skills which can be useful to you, and they'll appreciate being asked for their opinion. If you can sort out issues for an art director and make them look great to their boss and peers, they'll feel really positive about their decision to hire you – and they'll be happy to do it again.

Do:

- Communicate clearly
- Respond to questions and feedback in a timely way
- Deliver on time
- Offer your ideas and solutions
- Make the client aware of any issues that may affect the project as soon as possible.

Don't:

- Ask for more time on deadline day
- Disappear and stop communicating for days
- Change your idea, once a sketch has been approved – not unless you can communicate why you want to do so in good time and agree it with the client
- Struggle with an idea you can't make work. Ask for help!

Your first commissions

Every project will vary depending on the client, its urgency and type, but here's a typical outline of the process of taking a project from start to finish, so you can prepare for what to expect from your first commissions.

The enquiry

A client will contact you to ask if you're interested in working on their project. Typically, this is via email and in an ideal world, the client will send you all the details you need to know about the deliverables, schedule and, hopefully, the budget. (If they don't send you all the information, refer to Chapter 10 for a checklist of questions you can ask to gather what you need.)

Once you know everything you need to, you can:

- Make a decision whether the project is right for you
- Give the client your price, or
- Negotiate the budget (see Chapter 13 for more on negotiating).

You might also need to adjust the schedule or ask for a couple of extra days. Usually this is fine – if it's urgent, they'll tell you.

Sometimes, if a project is of a confidential nature, a client will send you a non-disclosure agreement (NDA) to sign before they can reveal any details (more on this in Chapter 14).

Always assume the client has contacted other illustrators about the project too. If you can make this first enquiry stage as quick and efficient as possible for the client, you'll reduce the chances of their hiring someone else while they're waiting for your answer. This doesn't mean you need to say 'Yes' immediately without giving it careful consideration; just that you should reply promptly and begin the conversation. Being the first to say 'Yes' to a project won't necessarily mean you'll win it – but being responsive and thoughtful in your reply demonstrates your professionalism.

The client may give you the green light right away, or take a few days to consider their options. If you don't hear back from them after three or four days, be sure to follow up to see if any decisions have been reached and to reaffirm your enthusiasm for the project.

It might be disappointing if you don't get the job; still, always reply to thank the client for their consideration and express your interest in working with them in the future. The fact that they were thinking of you for this one means you could win the next one, so it's best to stay friendly and positive.

The paperwork

Different clients will require you to fill in various forms to onboard you as a service provider to their company or organisation. Some may not need anything other than your invoice at the end, but bigger companies might request more information from you.

This could include:

- Tax forms – wherever you are, if you're working globally or cross-border, take some time to familiarise yourself with the tax rules in your own country and how they relate to working in other countries.
- For example, if you work with clients in the USA but aren't based there, you'll be required to fill out a W-8 BEN form,[26] which confirms that you are not a US taxpayer. After you've filled it out once, it can be used with all US clients, so you may want to do this in advance and keep it on file.
- If you're working from the UK with clients in the EU, you may need to apply for a certificate of residence[27] to claim tax relief with other countries, otherwise you might find your fee significantly reduced after double taxation.
- Banking information – the client needs to know how to pay you, so they might send you a form to fill in your bank details.
- New vendor information – this is usually simple information about you, such as address and contact details.

---

26   IRS (2023) 'About Form W-8 BEN, Certificate of Foreign Status of Beneficial Owner for United States Tax Withholding and Reporting'. Available at: www.irs.gov/forms-pubs/about-form-w-8-ben

27   UK Government (2015) 'How to apply for a certificate of residence to claim tax relief abroad', Corporation Tax, 2 December. Available at: www.gov.uk/guidance/get-a-certificate-of-residence

All of the above might be combined into one document or several. It's simply an admin task, so the client can create a record of you as a contributor.

- Usually you'll receive a contract or agreement that outlines the terms of the project (more on contracts in Chapter 14).
- Occasionally you may be required to send a picture of your passport or ID to show where you're based and eligible to work.
- In the UK, some organisations require freelancers to fill out an IR35 form.[28] This states that you are not an employee of the company or organisation, so they can prove they aren't responsible for your tax and national insurance contributions (or any other employee benefits).
- You may also receive a purchase order (PO). This is a form that companies generate to keep track of internal spending. It will have a PO number or code on it that you'll need to quote on your invoice: their finance team can then assign the invoice to the corresponding PO and process payment.

Ideally, you would receive all this paperwork before the project begins – especially the contract, as you need to know what you're agreeing to – but nobody is perfect, and an art director can occasionally forget to send you these things. They might even be slowed down by their legal department, who have to get the formal agreement ready (more on this in Chapter 14).

It can be frustrating when you send an invoice at the end of a project and only then receive the vendor onboarding forms, as that process can take some time. If you don't receive these things from the client upfront, ask if they have any forms they need you to complete – they'll appreciate the reminder.

I also strongly recommend you don't begin work until you've agreed the terms of the contract.

28   Brean Horne and Kristina Fox (2022) 'What is IR35 and what are IR35 rules?', *Nerdwallet*, 6 December. Available at: www.nerdwallet.com/uk/business-bank-accounts/guide-to-ir35/

Doing the job

Each illustrator's creative process is different, and clients need to see the work at key points as it progresses. Generally, this is in three basic stages:

1. First sketches
2. Refined version – usually with colour
3. Final image.

At each stage, the client has the opportunity to give feedback on the illustration. Three rounds of feedback are normal for a straightforward project, and this should be agreed with the client in advance to avoid too much back-and-forth.

As projects get more complicated and fees higher, the client might require more input through the process. For example, if you're working with an advertising agency, they might request two rounds of feedback from them, while their own client may also want two or three rounds. This is normal: the advertising agency wants to make sure the illustration is in a good place before they present it to their client; hopefully, in these situations the budget will be appropriately higher to accommodate those extra stages.

Let's look at these stages in more detail for a standard project.

First sketches

The client may only require one final illustration to be delivered, yet they might ask to see a few different ideas from which to choose. Sketches from illustrators can range from rough 'back of a napkin' doodles to fairly precise digital line drawings. As long as the samples communicate the idea clearly, they're doing their job for the purposes of this stage. If your sketches are particularly rough, you can also send some written notes to explain the idea. If the client asks for more than one sketched idea, two or three is reasonable. Any more than that should be negotiated as an additional fee.

The client should choose one idea to develop further and give you some notes to consider, as you move on to the next stage.

Refined version

This version will have moved away from a sketch: it could be digitally produced, include some more details and feature a preliminary colour palette. By now, the image should be taking shape to give the client a real taste of what they can expect the final image to look like. But crucially, you haven't gone too far down that path yet and started working on time-consuming finishing touches, as they'll want to offer more feedback before final delivery.

Final image

This is the finished piece. Once you reach the point where you're happy with the illustration, you can submit the 'final'. It's more than likely that the client will have some last comments and adjustments to make – but if all has gone to plan, these really should be minor tweaks.

Why the process works this way

The purpose of these stages is simply so that the art director or client can offer their input, which is usually helpful in making the illustration the best it can be; it's also so they can make sure nothing has been misunderstood.

Occasionally there is miscommunication and an artist ventures down a path that isn't in line with the project's goal – so having these regular check-ins avoids too much wasted time, should that happen. If you and your client aren't communicating and discussing the illustration at intermediate stages throughout the project, you run the risk of delivering what you *think* is the final, but *actually isn't* in line with the client's vision – which might require a lot of backtracking.

Always feel free to send a work-in-progress screenshot of the piece, if you need assistance or are unsure if you're on the right track – however, just be aware that this can invite more feedback and changes.

If the client makes major changes at the final stage, it means more work for you. In most cases, it's far easier to alter early sketches than the final image: encourage the client to give you plenty of feedback sooner in the process, so you can both avoid anything significant at the end.

Managing expectations

Some clients – usually the less experienced ones – are reluctant to let go of the reins: they want to check in with you and see your progress frequently. This is micromanaging, which comes partly from the client's lack of confidence in the illustrator's abilities, but mainly their own need to feel totally in control of all aspects of a project.

Not only does this interrupt your workflow, it also means they're likely to be constantly offering tiny adjustments and bits of feedback. As we'll explore later in this chapter, these small adjustments can add up to your having to give more time to the project than you bargained for.

How to handle a micromanager

If you find yourself working with a micromanaging client:

- Reassure them that you've understood their goal and can deliver what they need.
- Consider communicating more regularly than you ordinarily would, just to keep them in the loop – even if you're not showing them updates to the work.
- Explain that you need time to focus on the work, and that you'll be happy to share an update once you've reached the next stage.

It's more important to try and build up their trust in you and your skills, rather than challenging them by reminding them of your pre-agreed feedback stages, for example.

You don't need to confront their behaviour, just put their mind at ease. This soft skill comes in very handy when working with lots of different clients.

Generally speaking, it serves an illustrator well to be a little bit flexible and not split hairs over a few additional minor adjustments in the process – the client will appreciate it! But do consider whether each request is genuinely reasonable, or if it'll cause you a lot of extra work. If there are major, unexpected changes to the project which are outside of its scope, you'll need to tell the client that the fee needs to be adjusted accordingly to account for your extra time.

Delivery

Once you have client approval on the illustration, you can send the final file. The client might have specified what file type they need in the brief, or you might have asked them what they require.

Unless there's a legitimate reason to do so, don't send open, working files such as .ai or .psd formats with all your layers. While you might trust the art director you're working with, these files will end up in an archive somewhere. Having access to layers and individual elements only serves as temptation for someone else in the organisation to extract parts of the illustration to use separately, or adjust colours and move things around. It's possible the client might need some extra layers to integrate the illustration into a webpage, place title text in and among the illustration or perhaps animate the work. If that's been agreed, it's fine – but there aren't many other justifiable reasons for a client needing layered or open files.

If they do request layered or open files, ask what they intend to do with them. If it seems unnecessary, you can tell them it's not your usual practice to send working files. You don't need an excuse: they are your files. Even if they do have a good reason, ask which layers they need separating and deliver just that: this limits their access, and reduces temptation to alter your work.

You are the only person who should be making changes to your work – so a flattened .tif, .pdf or high-resolution .jpg usually suffices for most projects. As previously, be sure to discuss file requirements with your client. Clients making unauthorised changes to an illustrator's work doesn't happen a lot, but it's really frustrating when it does!

Once your final file has been approved, you can go ahead and invoice the client. Some art directors accept the invoice and pass it to their finance department, while others require you to send it directly to a specific accounts email address or department (this information usually appears on a PO, if you've received one).

Be sure to ask the art director if they need you to send the invoice elsewhere, and follow up if you don't receive confirmation – otherwise, you may not find out that the invoice wasn't submitted correctly until a month or so later, when you're expecting payment.

Make a good impression to get referrals

In other creative areas such as logo or web design, a potential client needing design work often asks their friends or contacts who designed their logo or website and gets a recommendation.

Referrals like this are so important to a lot of creative professionals, but they work a bit differently for freelance illustrators. If we're working primarily with companies and organisations instead of directly with an individual, it's unlikely that one advertising agency will ask another who they recommend. Unless an art director happens to be friends with a lot of other art directors, they may never be asked to recommend illustrators to other companies.

How to make referrals work for you

If you're doing great work with an art director at 'X Advertising' and make a good impression with your great ideas, creative input (and lovable personality!), you'll gain a fan. They'll hire you again when a suitable opportunity arises.

The next time they hire you, though, they might have moved to a different company, 'Y Agency'. They'll show your great work to their new creative director and recommend you because of what you made together in their previous role.

As you've already done excellent work with X Advertising, you'll be able to continue with them; it's a lot easier to do that if they know you've got a good track record there already. But you'll also gain credibility with Y Agency when the first art director sings your praises to their new employer.

When you've worked for X Advertising and Y Agency, you're showing you can do the job. The work you've made for X and Y will make 'Z Company' feel a lot more confident in hiring you.

Nobody's going to refer us if we don't do great work; but if we work with, say, 10 art directors in a year and create a meaningful impression, solve a problem for them or make their life easier, some of those people will move on to other roles and take us with them.

Art directors pride themselves on their network of skilled creatives: this is how your reputation can spread from company to company, even from industry to industry. An art director might begin at a magazine, move to a charity then perhaps an events company, and so on.

Even if you're working for big organisations, the personal connections you make can have enormous long-term value.

Good clients versus bad clients

At a certain point in your career, you'll want to find better clients to work with: it can mean more creative freedom, better reputation and deeper pockets. It's often the case that the first clients an illustrator works with are local businesses with high expectations and low budgets; but once they start to get work from bigger international clients, working for those local companies doesn't seem quite so attractive.

It's not unusual to feel like we owe our initial clients a favour if they gave us our first real projects, and to feel obligated to continue working with them. But if we fill our days with low-paying projects from demanding clients when we could be doing more interesting work with other ones, we'll be holding ourselves back. It can be damaging to our progress and motivation.

Whatever we think we may owe these early clients, it's not worth damaging our career over. They aren't doing us a favour by asking us to do work that's uninteresting and won't help us advance. Of course they want to keep us to themselves: if they can pay what we used to be worth as a beginner but get the high-quality work of a professional, they'll hold us back as long as possible.

A genuine supporter of your career recognises your skill and encourages you to seek out your dream clients – but unfortunately, in real life, that's unlikely to happen. Most clients make their own self-interest a priority, and so should you. You're no longer a student looking for work experience; you are running a business, so taking your future and professional development seriously is important.

It's never easy saying 'No' to people, especially regular clients – but we have to do it all through our career, as we work towards becoming the best we can be.

In *The Pumpkin Plan*,[29] small business author, Mike Michalowicz, ranks the three types of clients in this order:

1. Good clients
2. No clients
3. Bad clients.

When you have no clients, at least you have time to go out and look for good ones. But you can't do this if you're being kept busy by bad ones.

---

29   Mike Michalowicz (2012) *The Pumpkin Plan: A Simple Strategy to Grow a Remarkable Business in any Field*, Penguin Portfolio.

What is a bad client?

Over time, you'll be able to recognise the red flags for a bad client early on; but sometimes you won't find out until you're in the thick of a project – or even worse, when you're waiting for payment!

Here are some of the things that make for a bad client:

- Unclear communication about a project
- Unwillingness to consider your ideas or viewpoints
- Lack of respect for your time
- Not giving you timely feedback when you have a deadline to meet
- Unprofessional language or behaviour
- Persistent moving of project goalposts (more on this in 'What is scope creep?' below)
- Consistently giving you unreasonable timeframes for a project – occasionally deadlines are tight, it happens. But if it occurs every time, that shows a lack of forethought and planning on the client's part
- Unreasonable contract terms
- Micromanaging your every decision
- Late payment – or not paying at all!

Just as no one becomes a good illustrator without making mistakes and growing from them, a client might also need to learn how to be a good client. Sometimes you will find yourself frustrated by the people you work with.

I encourage you always to share your opinions and offer advice from an illustrator's viewpoint. It won't necessarily be taken on board, but that's the kind of creative a client wants on their team: someone who can spot problems and make a project the best it can be.

What is scope creep?

When you receive a client brief, it should have clearly defined objectives and deliverables (more on this in Chapter 10). When it does, you can plan your time and give them a price that's appropriate for that amount of work.

Sometimes though, as we've seen, a client can request minor amendments or additions throughout a project. Often the work evolves naturally as the client sees our sketches and thinks of new ideas, with reasonable give-and-take in the process. One or two new suggestions can actually improve the outcome, but do beware of a client who regularly asks for a little change here or an additional deliverable there, even if individually they won't take up much time. If this happens too frequently, you can find that what should have been a week-long project has turned into a three-week job – all that time adds up, and it can creep up on you without your noticing until it's too late and you're feeling frustrated.

Instead, decide what's reasonable: if a client consistently wants to change the project, make them aware that it may have an impact on cost. Often, clients don't realise they're doing it – so merely mentioning it will put a stop to it in most cases. If it doesn't, at least you can adjust your price accordingly.

Win better clients

There are plenty of great clients out there, and the only way we can get to work with them is by being so good that they won't want to consider the competition. Better clients are demanding – and they pay well. They want higher-quality illustration and better ideas, but they push us to do our best work too. The best clients respect our skill and opinions.

For example, when a great client is putting together an important advertising campaign, they want to work with exceptional talent – people who are enthusiastic and driven. A creative who doesn't really aspire to make exceptional work isn't an appealing partner for such a client.

If you want better clients, become the kind of illustrator a great client wants to work with – and know that you deserve them!

In the next chapter we'll be looking at what you can expect from client briefs.

Key takeaways

- Don't cause problems for a client – make their life easier.
- Make positive personal connections.
- Get the paperwork out of the way before you begin the project.
- Agree revision rounds before the project begins.
- If working with foreign countries, find out if the client needs any tax or other essential information from you early, as this can take some time to complete.
- Watch out for scope creep. Those small changes really add up!
- If your days are filled with bad clients, you don't have time to find better ones.
- Look out for bad client red flags.
- Win better clients by being the best illustrator you can be.

10

How to deal with client briefs

What is a brief?

When you're hired for a project, you'll receive a brief: it's your list of instructions from the client for the job they'd like you to do, including the necessary information you'll need to complete it. It can be written out in a document, or discussed over a call or in person.

If initially the project is discussed on a call, be sure to ask for a written brief: partly because it's easier to see all the information you need in one document or email, and partly to avoid any potential for disagreement or misunderstanding about what was spoken about or agreed during the call.

Typically, a client brief includes:

- Background information on the client and/or company
- Information on the particular project
- Technical specifications
- Reference images
- A mood board or examples of an illustration style that the client likes
- A page layout
- The schedule
- A list of required deliverables
- The licence required
- The budget
- And most importantly, a description of what they would like you to do.

Let's look at these in more detail.

Information on the company

Sometimes this information isn't necessary to complete the job, but it does give you an idea of:

- The customers the client is serving
- The areas of the market they are in
- Their goals and values.

Take a look at the client's website to get a picture of who they are and what they do.

Information on the project

Every project has a goal: you need to know what that is, so you can focus your efforts in the right place. For example, if the brief is for an event poster, you would need to find out:

- What kind of event it is
- What sort of people will be attending
- The scale of the event
- The purpose of the event
- How and where the poster will be used – if, say, it's only going to be used on social media at small scale, your approach might be very different to producing an A1 print to appear in an event space.

Technical specifications

These are the nuts and bolts of the project, what the printer or designer needs to receive from you to do their part of the job properly:

- Size – what does the client need the poster to be?
- Resolution – if it's only being used digitally, what's required will be different from a print application.
- File type – what does the client need, e.g. .jpg, .pdf, .psd, .ai, .tif? (See also Chapter 9.)

- Any restrictions – for example, print medium: is the poster being screen-printed? There may be restrictions on how many colours you can use.

Reference images

If the client wants you to draw something specific, such as a piece of technical equipment, an exotic plant or particular model of yacht, you'll need them to send some decent photos for you to see what it looks like.

Note that these are for reference only: they're not to be copied unless the client tells you otherwise and has the necessary rights and permission. (Usually these images are gathered from a quick internet search, so the client won't have the rights to use them.)

Mood board and examples

When the client has seen something they like, they often send a few images as inspiration: this is a useful way to check you're both on the same page. If they haven't sent you any, asking for examples could save you a lot of back-and-forth trying to work out what they're envisioning.

They might also send an example from your own portfolio and ask you to make something similar. This is helpful for the project, but also useful information as you develop your portfolio – if your clients are referencing certain images frequently, they're telling you what you're good at!

A layout

A magazine, publisher or graphic designer may have already laid out the text and other elements on the page, and assigned a space for the illustration you're making. If so, they can send a .pdf of the layout for you to see the space you have to play with for it.

The schedule

Most projects have a deadline by whch the client needs to receive the final deliverables from you. Occasionally, a client will say there's no fixed end-date: if they do this, you can suggest one that works with your current workload. However, I'd always encourage you to set a deadline, just to make sure the project doesn't go on too long; also to ensure that you and the client are aligned as to what's going to be delivered and when. Usually, client deadlines are somewhat flexible: if you think you might need a few extra days on the project, it's better to ask right at the beginning rather than later.

As we saw in Chapter 9, the client will want to see sketches or work-in-progress stages throughout the project; some also ask for a lot of check-ins, which can be disruptive to your work schedule, but it's reasonable for them to want to see how it's going. You can always negotiate the timeline to give the client enough updates and keep them happy, but not so many that you spend more time waiting for their feedback than actually doing the work.

The deliverables

This is what you'll be sending in your final hand-off to the client on deadline day.

Continuing the event poster example above, this could include for example:

- 1 x A2 size, portrait, print resolution .tif file
- 1 x 9:16 ratio version, for use on social media
- 1 x 1:1 ratio version, also for social media
- Any uncommon font files you may have used in the design.

The licence required

Although a licence isn't technically required for you to make the work, it's often included at this stage to give you a full picture of the project, so you can send your price.

We'll look at licences in more detail in Chapter 14, but essentially these cover:

- How your work can be used by the client
- Where it can be used
- How long it can be used for.

The budget

Again, a figure isn't necessary in itself for you to complete the work, but it is essential to know if you're deciding whether or not to take the job. (More on budgets and pricing in Chapter 13.)

What the client wants

Our interpretation of a project can differ from a client's vision, so we need them to communicate clearly what their goal is. Armed with this information, we can apply our skills in a way that's useful to them. Two people reading a newspaper article can take away completely different meanings, based on their respective backgrounds and experience. Similarly, the client can tell us what points they consider important enough to be worth highlighting in an illustration.

For example, with an article or book chapter, you might be given the text and asked to illustrate it with no additional information: in this case, it's worth asking the client which points they consider the most important. This shows the client that you're considering *their* goal for the project and *their* readers, rather than simply interpreting it from your own viewpoint.

They might also give you a theme: 'We'd like this event poster to evoke a summer holiday feeling', or a tone: 'This article deals with a delicate, mental health subject, so should be represented seriously.'

On the following pages is an example of a clear and well-written brief.

Example illustration brief

What we need

Illustrations for a cocktail menu for a bar called Drinks 'r' Us. The bar is located in a new hotel called The Five Star Hotel, opening in Shanghai this September.

Schedule

- 30 May – first sketches
- 3 June – feedback from client
- 6 June – second draft/revisions
- 9 June – feedback from client
- 12 June – final delivery.

Technical details

- Book size: A5 (148mm x 210mm)
- 15 x 1 colour spot illustrations required (no larger than 6–8cm)
- As the menu is still being developed, we need illustrations that are slightly generic, so they can be used across different drinks. They are typically identified by the glassware used.

Illustration list (feel free to suggest others):

- Group of drinks on a tray
- Punchbowl with glasses
- Cocktails in the following glasses:

    o Margarita
    o Hurricane
    o Highball
    o Shot
    o Martini
    o Champagne flute

- Wine glasses and bottles
- Cocktail shaker.

Deliverables

High-resolution 300dpi (minimum) .tif files (so we can change the colour on the page, depending on the paper colour chosen by the client).

Style

The client liked these stock illustration options:

We think this style could work better:

Overall, we're looking for cocktails in a simple vintage style similar to a linocut, but still with a slight hand-drawn texture to it. The menu is inspired by Art Deco cocktail books of that era, with 'speakeasy'-style drinks.

The illustrations will be used throughout the menu/book, possibly on some other small marketing collateral associated with the bar. It's a high-end, beautiful bar space designed by architects in London and New York.

Briefs come in all shapes and sizes

I've seen briefs as simple as a couple of sentences or a very rough sketch from an art director; I've also seen corporate documents more than 50 pages-long, with so much unnecessary information it's hard to know where to begin! The former requires an illustrator to ask the client a lot of questions, while the latter forces them to weed out the essentials and ignore the rest.

Not every brief includes all the items listed above: some will be unnecessary for one project and vital for another; but there are essential things for you to know to be able to give an accurate price and complete the project.

If the brief you receive doesn't have what you need, it's fine to ask for it. Your client might not be aware of what you need to know to do your part – so they either miss bits or throw everything at you and hope for the best. They'll appreciate your guidance, once you've taken the time to consider what you need from them.

Ask lots of questions

As an illustrator, you aren't expected to read an art director's or author's mind: the only way you can do your best work is by fully under-standing the brief, article or goal of the project. Since new illustrators lack experience, it's understandable that you might feel a bit insecure about this: that you shouldn't ask too many questions in case the client thinks you don't know what you're doing. But you don't need to be an expert in every subject you illustrate, or able to interpret a company's corporate goals.

If you aren't clear about something, just go ahead and ask the client. Professionals avoid guessing and are comfortable with asking as many questions as necessary to fully comprehend the project: then, they can go ahead and do the job to the best of their ability as a result.

Producing something the client doesn't want because we didn't ask enough questions is a far worse option: so, the more we know about a project, the better our work will be. As we've just seen, the client doesn't necessarily know what we need to know, so it's our job to get the information we need.

Client brief checklist

If the client doesn't have a brief, here's a checklist of sample questions you can ask to help them construct one for you. Just tailor the questions to the specific project.

- [ ] How will the illustration be used – e.g. book cover, website banner, billboard or all of the above?

- [ ] What is the illustration for – what is its purpose, to attract more customers or help explain an idea?

- [ ] What actions do you want people to take, or what do you want them to think about when they see it?

- [ ] Who is the target audience – how old are they, what are they interested in, where do they live?

- [ ] What size, shape and resolution do you want the illustration to be?

- [ ] What key points do you want to highlight in the image – is there a specific brand message or concept I should focus on?

- [ ] What style do you like? If you have any reference images or illustrations you like, please do send them over.

Calls and video chats with clients

To brief the illustrator

Often, higher-paying clients ask you to jump on a video call at the beginning of a project so they can brief you: 90% of the time, these calls consist of introductions to the team – the art director, designer and producer, etc. Then the client proceeds to read through the briefing document they've already sent you by email, and doesn't offer much additional information other than what you've already read yourself.

What's the point of this? First, it's for the client to speak to you in person and get a better sense of you than they can from an email. Second, it's an opportunity for you to ask any of the above questions that the written brief doesn't answer. Third – and this almost never happens – it's an opportunity for you to 'wow' the client, and make it clear to them you're the right person for their project.

To find the right illustrator

Sometimes, these calls happen before the client has chosen the illustrator they want to commission. The thing is, if we just sit there, nod along and don't ask any questions, not only are we not getting anything out of the interaction, we're not offering the client anything they couldn't have gathered from our website.

Many illustrators see that the client wants a briefing call and think: 'I don't need to read the brief in detail, if they're going to talk me through it' – but this is your opportunity to make a great impression and win the client!

Wow the client

When our illustrator Alex joins a video call with three or four people from the client's design team, instead of awkwardly waiting in that opening silence that often happens, he's proactive:

'Hey, it's great to meet you all! I'm really excited to hear more about the project and discuss some ideas with you.'

They do a round of introductions, then the client shares their screen and starts talking through each slide. Alex has some pre-prepared questions he wants to ask for certain pages, so he says to the client:

'I've read through the brief in detail, so we don't have to go through every page, but I do have a few questions on pages 3 and 5.'

This saves everybody's time and gets to the important parts that help Alex do his job. When it comes to the pages describing what the client wants, Alex says:

'Is it okay if I share my screen, because I'd love to show you a couple of ideas I've started sketching?'

He pulls them up for the client, then offers a time plan of what he will do in weeks 1, 2 and so on, as well as when he can deliver key stages of the project for the client to review.

Now the client is invested. What kind of illustrator starts sketching ideas before they've won the job? The right one!

Now, sketching out a couple of quick ideas might mean that Alex has worked for an hour for free; but when he joins this call, he already has something to talk about with the client and is demonstrating value. Whether the sketches are right at this stage isn't important, because what they're actually providing is an opportunity to discuss them and get some quick feedback. This shows the client how:

- An illustrator thinks
- Professionally they can present themselves and their ideas
- Enthusiastic they are
- Much better a fit they are for the client's creative team than the other illustrators they're considering.

I've sat in on a lot of calls like this, and that confident, proactive preparation almost never happens. But when it does, it allows both artist and client to skip past the time-wasting chit-chat and get right into the project. When they can do that, they're already working on developing it together – the client is invested in the artist. They've instantly separated themselves from everyone else. Just imagine how much easier the fee negotiation will be, once the client is already hooked!

It isn't always necessary to go over-and-above in this way – but if you do find yourself with an opportunity to wow a great client, take it.

Exercise: Brief yourself

While an illustrator is learning the ropes and building their portfolio, often they'll set themselves projects. This is a great way to practise and begin thinking like your clients do.

If you're still on your way to finding your first clients or want to round out your portfolio, try using this chapter to write yourself a brief. It may be easy to think about a simple format, such as a full- or half-page illustration – but if you want to add some variety to your pieces, why not set yourself some interesting restrictions and challenges?

How about these?

- Do you always work in full colour – why not limit yourself to four, or two? Some printing methods require restricted colours.
- Rather than working to a full-frame image where your illustration fills the given rectangular dimensions, can you try a more organic background shape?
- What different ideas can you come up with for the same project description, but aimed at two different demographics? For example, what works for a student could be quite different from what a forty-something parent of three would like.
- Imagine the client is printing on coloured paper – what adjustments would you have to make to your work, so that it looks good?

These are just a few examples. Illustration can be applied in so many interesting and unusual formats that the only limit is your imagination of what a commercial project could require of you. This will help you view an illustration commission from both sides of the brief.

In the next few chapters, we're going to switch gears and look into different aspects of your freelance business, starting with developing good financial habits.

Key takeaways

- Consider what you need to know to do the job.
- Read the brief carefully.
- The client may not know what you need – if a brief doesn't have enough information, be sure to ask for it.
- If you have an opportunity to wow a client with your preparation and enthusiasm, take it!
- Set yourself some interesting constraints to add variety to your portfolio.
- Practise writing briefs for self-initiated projects.

11

Managing your money

Using your money wisely

Money is a problem when we don't have enough of it – and if we're
embarking on a new career, the chances are that it'll be on our mind.
Being sensible with money is an absolutely essential trait for freelancers
throughout their career, so it pays to develop good financial habits as
early as you can.

If you have savings, you'll want to make them last as long as
possible; if you don't, you'll need to find ways to cut costs. It won't
always be possible to save, but if you can squirrel away part of your
earnings and keep outgoings low, there will be less pressure when you
haven't had a paying client in a few weeks.

As we touched on in Chapter 3, there are some things an illustrator
needs to do the job (computer, website, etc.), but you don't need the
latest equipment or an expensive website. If you can find space to work
at home, there's no need to rent a studio; you can work from anywhere
and be contactable and responsive, so living in an expensive city isn't
necessary either. You don't even need a formal qualification, because
you can train yourself in illustration for next to nothing by using online
resources and getting feedback from industry professionals.

It's true that you can't get much for free, but you can keep costs low
if you use your money wisely. Some things you will need to buy, while
others may be worth paying for, if you can afford them (such as online
learning platforms or membership of the Association of Illustrators).

Don't spend before you're earning

A trap that some new illustrators fall into, when they're trying to find
their first clients, is thinking they have to spend a lot on self-promotion.

There are many things we could outlay on to get our name out there:

- Printed promotional materials – postcards, business cards, mini-portfolios, prints, etc.
- Illustration annuals – e.g. *Workbook*, *Directory of Illustration*, etc.
- Custom-built websites
- Buying lists of contacts.

As an illustrator, you could spend a lot of money in the first few months attempting to get your work in front of the right people (I speak from experience!); but while these things have their place, they aren't necessarily a good investment for new artists.

A lot of illustrators who pay large amounts to be listed in illustration annuals don't have a commercially viable style – they've wasted their money. If they haven't had their work validated before doing this, the expensive printed promotional items they send off to clients and agents will go straight in the bin because their work isn't good enough. And if that work isn't to a professional standard yet, a meeting with a well-meaning client isn't going to result in paid work either.

There are lists of client contacts available to buy, but every other new artist has those too: if those contacts are so easily available, the competition will be high.

Spending a lot of money before you know whether your work is right is a complete gamble. If you're not making money from illustration yet, save your limited funds and use the one good resource you do have: time. Spend it wisely, by making your work better and getting in touch with potential clients directly.

Quick and cheap self-promotion

The best form of self-promotion for a beginner is the cheapest and quickest: email. Social media is cheap, but we've established that it can take a long time to build a following and get our work seen by the right people; this simply adds an unnecessary step when we could be sending our work straight to real clients.

And as we've just seen above, sending out printed postcards or promotional items is expensive (and doesn't necessarily work for new artists anyway). Many potential clients will be working from home, so they may never see things posted to their office – but they'll definitely see an email.

Once you're getting regular work from clients you've won via direct contact, you've proved to yourself that your illustration work is commercially viable and you are getting paid for it – that's when you can be confident that investment in self-promotion won't be wasted. If your work is good enough for your first few clients, it'll be good enough for others.

When to quit the day job

It's common for illustrators to have a day (or evening) job while building their portfolio and client list. At a certain point – generally after saving up enough to live on for around six months – they might decide to go full-time and give it their best shot. Quitting a day job so we can give illustration our full attention might seem like the best course of action, but it's also important to consider the financial realities.

It takes time to build a sustainable freelance business, and there's no way to tell how long it might take to find those first clients. All the time that we're plugging away at illustration, our savings will be running out.

It's no easy task to save up enough to live on, even for a few months. It's important to ask yourself: what would I do if I ran out of money? We also need to consider our motivation while we've had a day job: have we been consistent in our efforts with illustration? If it's been difficult to stay that way part-time, are we sure we can commit to it full-time? It's hard to stay motivated, working full-time at something, when we're not getting an income from it. We won't necessarily feel like doing it every day, and every day that we do miss extends the time it takes to reach that goal.

Quitting a job to go and work on something untested is a risk – so don't leave one that pays the bills until you're sure that freelance illustration can support you. Instead, work on illustration part-time alongside it and test the water before jumping in head first. If you can commit to that – even for just few hours a week – it'll help you develop discipline and the ability to stick with a routine, both of which are crucial for your success as a freelancer.

Once you've started finding paid work, you'll know freelance illustration is a viable option: when clients are willing to pay you enough to live on as a part-time illustrator, you can make the leap to full-time more confidently. If you've been consistently working part-time on your illustrations for a year and still haven't found any paying clients, going full-time isn't likely to change that. This suggests that time isn't what is holding you back.

It takes time to reach a point where creative pursuits can support you financially, so having a day job as a safety net is vital. You need to know you can make money from illustration before taking that leap.

While a decent day job will take away some of your time, it provides you with financial stability and a schedule around which you can plan your creative work. Time constraints can be helpful too: if you give yourself, say, an entire week to work on an illustration, it will probably take that long; but if you only have an hour a day, you'll be forced to cut out non-essentials and distractions to make progress.

My day job

If a day job drains our energy and makes it hard to motivate ourselves for creative work, we need to consider finding a different one that allows for better balance.

When I was beginning my freelance illustration career, I had a job in a bar, working early evening through to early hours. I liked the work – it was fun and social! – but exhausting. I worked long shifts and wouldn't get home until past 2am most nights, sometimes later.

This meant I would roll into my studio to work on illustration at midday, then have to check out again around 4pm. It didn't mean I couldn't get anything done, but it was extremely difficult to get into a creative mindset. Not only that, but a sociable work environment naturally led to spending the money I was supposed to be saving!

After several months of this pattern, I found myself needing to find a better job that could support my new business. It was fun working in the bar, but it held me back from making progress in my career. Eventually I did find a better balance, but my progress was much slower than it could have been.

Working for free

It's common for freelance illustrators to be asked to work for free, or in exchange for 'exposure', all the way through their careers by all kinds of people, companies and causes. These people are out to get something for nothing – and often they can get it; that's why they keep doing it. If a company asks a number of illustrators to do something for free, unfortunately some of them will say 'Yes'.

Even if doing a real project isn't paid, its appeal to a new illustrator is that it's a challenge and change of pace to working on self-initiated projects (which is also work you're doing for free). It's a chance to make a good impression on a potential future client, and it's possible that the final product might expose your work to other potential paying clients.

The consequences of working for free

If an aspiring illustrator wants to be part of the creative industry, they should seriously consider how their decisions and actions affect it – because if creatives continue to work for free, it perpetuates the idea that this kind of work isn't valuable. That's a heavy burden for a new artist to take on.

Every person has the right to make up their own mind whether they should offer their services for free, but they should only make that decision if they have taken the time to inform themselves about the possible consequences – and have seriously considered the pros and cons. If every illustrator were to take that responsibility, it wouldn't necessarily mean that *all* illustrators would say 'No' to working for free; but it would mean they were able to judge each case on its merits and make an informed decision.

If an illustrator can see a genuine opportunity to advance their career by offering their services for free and they don't take it, no one will thank them for it. If they do go ahead with it after giving it the consideration it deserves – and using their best, well-informed judgement – I don't see that anybody has a right to challenge them on it.

If there's a cause you care about and want to donate your time to, by all means do it: you get to decide how you spend your time. But other clients – commercial and corporate – will ask you as a creative to work for free too.

Exchange of value

The idea of working for free is something that inspires a lot of passionate argument, mainly along the lines of 'Never do it'. This is an overly simple conclusion to a complicated problem.

If a client is getting value from the work we provide to them, they should be willing to pay us for that value. If they won't pay but are offering something else in return that helps us advance or develop, we have to decide if what we're getting back is worth the trade. There still needs to be an exchange of value even if it isn't monetary. For example, if a web designer offers to build our website in exchange for a logo design, that might be both a fair trade and an opportunity to recommend them to others, and vice versa.

However, if a company with no following to speak of or connections to whom they could recommend you says, 'There'll be great exposure from this project!', ask them specifically how they plan to promote you to other potential paying clients. Most of them can't answer – they're simply trying to take advantage.

But if, for example:

- Your name will appear prominently wherever the work is shown
- They'll tag you in a social media post to their 500,000 followers
- They'll write up an article about you on their high-traffic website
- They're going to organise a meeting where you can pitch your work to their partners or different departments in the company

– that is a legitimately good opportunity.

However, a company which has these kinds of connections can almost certainly afford to pay you – if they choose to do so. When a global corporation says it doesn't have a budget for the work, it's because it's *choosing* not to allocate funds to creatively develop a project, *not* because that money doesn't exist.

A valuable opportunity

None of the TED speakers are paid to do talks, but if an author or expert were asked to do one, they'd be foolish to turn it down. They can provide a valuable presentation to the TED platform and its viewers, and in return they'll get genuinely great publicity and social proof that they're an expert in their field.

Normally these those authors and experts might charge thousands to speak at an event, but they know that what they'll get back from doing a free TED talk is far more useful than a one-off fee.

Exercise: Should I work for free?

Here are a few questions to ask yourself when a company or person asks you to work for free.

1. Why aren't they offering me any money?
    This is something you should ask them directly.
2. Can't they afford it?
    If they can't, they probably can't offer you much else in return either.
3. If it's a charity, is the person asking also working for free?
4. Are they paying other people to work on the project – are the graphic designer or photographer being paid, and if they are, why not the illustrator?
5. Do other similar companies pay for this kind of work – if they do, how can this company justify not paying?
6. Will I have creative freedom?
    If you do, you might enjoy it; but if the client is going to be very demanding and won't be paying you, it's not worth it.
7. Is this company going to make money from the value I provide to the project?
    If your work is good, the answer is probably yes; but if it's for a non-profit or charitable event, maybe not.
8. Am I going to learn anything from working on the project?
    If you have the opportunity to develop your skills, learn from other great creatives and work on a project that's more complicated and interesting than anything you've done before, you might get a lot out of it.
9. If they aren't offering money, what else can they offer me?
    Free tickets, products, gift vouchers? These are all things you might find valuable.
10. Will this project actually lead to anything else?
    Ask what other illustration projects they work on regularly.
11. Does this company have other projects for which they pay illustrators?
    If you do a good job it could lead to other work; but a client that has paid you for your work is more likely to value it and take you seriously in the future.

> 12. Will this project give me great exposure?
>   Most of the time, it's a no.

How to make more money

There are a few options to make more money from your illustrations.

Get more clients

As a new artist your focus will be on getting *some* clients, then *more* until you're busy. As we've seen, at the beginning many of your clients will be on the lower-paying end of the spectrum; if your time is packed with the ones who don't pay all that well, you'll reach a cap on how much you can earn.

Work longer hours

You can always work 15-hour days to fit in more projects, but clearly this isn't a sustainable way to operate. There will be occasional late nights as deadlines loom, but that isn't something to aim for as a regular practice or long-term strategy, because it can lead to burn-out.

Get quicker

If you can work faster, you can take on more projects. Efficiency is good, but there's a limit to how much work you can do: working as quickly as you can probably won't lead to the best creative output.

Raise your prices

Some of your existing clients won't be able to afford you if you increase your rates. However, if some of them are willing to pay more, you could earn the same amount by doing less work. In that case, it isn't necessarily worth holding on to the lowest-paying clients.

Find better clients

This is the best option by far. As we discovered in Chapter 9, better clients can ask a lot of us, but they respect the way we work – and they pay well.

Simply working harder, faster and longer is an antiquated way of looking at career progression. It doesn't necessarily mean the work is any good, and doing more for low-paying clients doesn't push us to be the best we can be either.

It's only by finding the best clients who need higher-quality work that you'll be able to develop as an illustrator, while also earning what you're worth. Clients are paying for the value you can add to their project: if you can add a lot of that, you can charge a lot.

In the next chapter we'll move on to look at your new freelance business.

Key takeaways

- Don't spend too much before you're earning money from illustration.
- Email is the cheapest and quickest form of self-promotion.
- Find a job that supports your illustration career and doesn't hold you back.
- Don't quit your day job before you're making money from illustration.
- If you're asked to work for free, consider all the pros and cons.
- The best way to make more money is to find better clients.

12

A freelancer is a business

Building your freelance business

Institutional education in the creative arts can leave a lot to be desired when it comes to running a business: as a result, many new illustrators graduate without the essential knowledge to turn their creative skills into a thriving enterprise. Unfortunately, this can leave them feeling unprepared for the commercial world; so new creative freelancers need to discover these skills independently to give them the best shot at success.

Thankfully, abundant resources are available online for small business owners and freelancers, not to mention decades' worth of fantastic books on related subjects (see the Further resources). Often these skills are picked up as a freelancer makes their way through their first few years in business, which is a perfectly reasonable way to do it. You can learn the skills as you need them, but getting into the mindset of a business owner from Day 1 will change the way you view freelance illustration. Your priorities move from the creative process to considering:

- What your clients want from you
- How you present yourself to the world
- How you interact with people
- How you spend your time.

The bottom line is that if a creative freelancer doesn't behave like a businessperson, they won't be treated like one. Their time won't be respected, they probably won't be paid fairly, and their clients will control the direction of their career when the freelancer should be in the driver's seat.

Here are a few things to consider – some of which we've already discussed in detail – but they're worth repeating here:

- You need a steady flow of work – prospect for new clients, even when you're busy. If you're not doing this regularly, you'll be more vulnerable to extended quiet periods.
- Keep an eye on your finances:

  o How much are you spending?
  o Are your clients paying on time?
  o Are you invoicing on time?
  o Are you putting aside an amount for your taxes (and any other essential contributions) from every project?

- Nurture your business relationships – make a good impression on clients and when a project is completed, don't forget to keep in touch with them.
- Be adaptable – if what you're doing isn't making money, something needs to change. Be realistic about the sustainability of your career, and change course if necessary.
- Think long-term – if you don't know where you want to be in five years, how can you plan to get there? Not every project you are offered will get you closer to your goal.
- Be purposeful and deliberate – choose to work towards creating a portfolio of work that you want to do more of and fills you with pride. If you're swept along by things that other people want you to do, you might end up somewhere you don't want to be.
- Focus on the essentials – use your time at work to its maximum potential. Concentrate on the activities that propel you forward, rather than lead you in circles.
- You are not your business – many freelancers don't have healthy boundaries with work: they do too much and burn out. Look after yourself first, and your business second.

A freelance illustrator can get by with a basic knowledge of small business operation, and many choose to stick at that level – but they're barely scratching the surface. They could thrive and leap ahead of the competition with further investment in the right business skills:

- An illustrator who can sell, or market their work better than others has a considerable advantage in finding and winning clients.
- Someone who can manage their time well and systematise their workflow will be more productive.
- An illustrator who can communicate their vision to clients will be rewarded with more satisfying work (more on this in the next section).
- If an illustrator can negotiate well, they'll make more money.

Communicate effectively

As an illustrator, you're a communicator: your creative work conveys the client's ideas and intentions; if it doesn't, it won't be doing its job properly. Your illustration style is the method you use to deliver messages. An illustrator also needs to communicate their own ideas to the client and show them how they will solve their problem. Developing the art of communicating ideas is different from developing a style, so every good illustrator needs to acquire both skills.

An illustrator may be exceptional at communicating visually, but it's possible their clients may think entirely differently. The thought process of a creative is likely to be quite different to that of a corporate professional, for example – so a professional illustrator develops different kinds of communication skills to be able to:

- Listen to what the client wants to achieve
- Interpret a brief by reading carefully and asking the right questions
- Demonstrate to the client how they can solve their problem – which could be in the form of visuals, but also written explanations or presentations.

A client may or may not know what they want, so a good illustrator is able to ask the right questions and draw out the key goals of a project for those clients (for more on this, see the Client brief checklist in Chapter 10), as well as those who do.

If the client doesn't understand an idea or why it might benefit the project, it's not going to be taken seriously – so it is important to develop the skills you need to present your ideas effectively, such as:

- Sketching in a way that's clear for a non-creative professional to comprehend
- Explaining your ideas in writing to supplement the sketches
- Practise talking through your ideas before you speak with a client
- Tell the client why this idea will appeal to their target demographic
- Point out the key features and explain why they are important in catching a customer's eye.

If you can't explain your ideas or sell them to the client, then they're of no value to you or the client.

In many cases, an art director working with a corporate client can be the bridge to the creative world; but an illustrator who also possesses these communication skills can truly understand what a client wants – even when the client has a different communication style.

Be your own salesperson

A lot of new illustrators are resistant to selling their own work: if our illustrations are largely untested in a commercial environment, it's understandable that we might feel some insecurity about selling them. We don't want to annoy people by contacting them to offer our services, and we might feel uncomfortable talking about money because we aren't sure what realistic budgets are.

As we saw in Chapter 2, it's possible we might be feeling impostor syndrome or wondering why a reputable client would want to pay for our work – which leads to quoting far too low for our services (we'll look at this in more detail in the next chapter).

Selling our work and ideas is a skill that every creative must develop, but 'sales' does have a bit of an anti-creative feel to it. We might be thinking: *I don't want to be a nuisance,* or *They'll think I only care about money.* This is common in new freelancers and business owners, who end up pricing their services low so they don't have to learn how to sell clients on the value of their work.

Believe in your own product and skill, so you can tell the client why your plan is going to meet their needs. Your portfolio is proof that you've done that for other projects – but also bear in mind that the client can't see the creative process, or how you work, from the final outcome. What they're hiring you for is your style, but also your expertise: being able to explain ideas and key benefits effectively could be what convinces them to hire you over another illustrator.

Freelance illustrators are rarely asked to present their work to a client: most likely it'll be emailed to an art director or design agency, then they'll pass it on for someone else to present to the end client. It's crucial to send written explanations of your ideas along with your sketches, so the person presenting your work has everything they need to sell the work on your behalf.

Making well-researched work for a particular audience is providing something they want rather than what the illustrator wants; and if we're solving creative problems effectively for a particular industry, then selling our work to them will be a lot easier. Clients will no longer be doing you a favour by taking a chance on your work; you'll be doing them a favour by showing them work they can actually use.

Offer your expertise

A good illustrator's expertise can result in stunning visuals – but naturally, it doesn't begin and end with that. They know what works and can suggest ideas and improvements to a client, based on their skill and knowledge.

If an illustrator is too afraid of giving their opinion, they aren't offering the full scope of what a great client wants. Ultimately, their ideas for a project might not be used by the client; but again, if they can present them in a way that the client can understand and appreciate, they'll be given fair consideration.

What makes a professional

While many amateur illustrators are trying to make it into a career, there are few true professional illustrators. An amateur illustrator can solve a problem for a client who knows exactly what they want, but a professional can assess a project and figure out what the client needs. They look deeper than the written brief, providing something to the client that not only meets their immediate needs, but opens up opportunities and improves their own offer to their customers.

The qualities of a professional

We've looked at some of these already, but here are the qualities that make a true professional illustrator.

They:

- Understand what their clients want – they define their target audience and make work that's useful for them.
- Don't compromise on quality – delivering low-quality work isn't an option for a professional. What they put out into the world has meaning, and they hold themselves to a high standard.
- Share their point of view – the best clients want illustrators who share their specialist skill and knowledge. Combining the client's needs and the illustrator's expert guidance takes a project to another level.
- Are knowledgeable in their field – they pay attention to trends and technology, and can advise a client on what will or won't work.

- Take a long-term view – they understand that things like winning the best clients and building a great portfolio take time, and are patient.
- Are paid fairly for their time and skill – most people have no idea if they're being paid fairly. Professionals do the research and find out.
- Are adaptable – they aren't too precious about ideas or techniques, because they know they have the skills to produce more ideas and acquire new techniques. They understand that they'll have both busy and quiet periods, and can use their time effectively either way.
- Commit to continuous professional development – they know that most others don't do this, so the skills they gain over the years become increasingly valuable.
- Are confident in their offer – a professional illustrator knows where their strengths lie, and uses them to their full potential.
- Are honest about what they can't offer – if they can't deliver what the client needs, they're upfront about it so the client can move on and find the best fit for the project.
- Are organised – this saves time, which means producing more great work (or taking a day off whenever they feel like it!).
- Are proactive – they don't wait for the next project to land in their inbox. They reach out to new clients consistently, so their flow of work is as steady as possible.
- Are dependable and predictable – dependable always, and predictable in the level of quality they deliver.
- Ask questions – a professional isn't satisfied with superficial understanding of a project. The more they can learn about the client's goals and the subject, the better their work will be.
- Have developed all the skills a freelancer needs – the creative part is a large piece of the puzzle, but many more are needed to do the job to a professional level.

In addition to all of these, a professional is reasonable and flexible. They understand that it won't always be possible to do everything they want to within a project. They're willing to compromise where they can, but aren't afraid to stand firm on the things they believe to be important either – this requires self-belief and integrity.

In the next chapter we're going to get to grips with pricing and negotiating.

Key takeaways

- Familiarise yourself with how to run a small business from Day 1.
- Change how you communicate, depending on the client.
- Take the time to really understand your client's goal for the project.
- Offer your opinion and expertise.
- Sell the client on the value you can offer.
- Be confident in what you can offer, and honest about what you can't.
- Professional illustrators are dependable, proactive and organised.
- Be reasonable and flexible.

13

Pricing your work and negotiating

Treat pricing as an experiment

There's no way around it: pricing work becomes easier with experience. It's impossible for a book or website to give you an accurate price to quote for your work: one that tells you to quote £X for a certain kind of illustration can only ever be a general guide. It doesn't:

- Factor in your financial circumstances
- Know how complex or time-consuming your illustration style is
- Take the client's budget into consideration.

For example, if we quote £700 as a standard price for a full-page magazine illustration, we'll be way too high for some magazines and much too low for others. Every client has a different budget, and there is no single right answer. Unfortunately, this often means that pricing our work in the early days of our career can be frustrating.

Pricing is one of the biggest issues for a new illustrator: it's your living after all, and many worries and insecurities go along with putting a price on your own skills. You will make mistakes along the way, but it's how you'll grasp costing your work accurately. You might lose the occasional job by quoting too high, and leave money on the table by quoting too low. But over time you'll get to know what different kinds of clients pay for illustration, also how much work that different kinds of projects require. A low-paying client doesn't necessarily mean an easier project.

Because there is no one-size-fits-all pricing model, every illustrator has to figure it out as they go and treat it as an experiment. Every miscalculation becomes new data that helps you work out how to price accurately.

The three P's of pricing

Here's a handy rule-of-thumb model. When you're considering taking on any project, it should have at least two of these three P's:

- Price – if you're getting a good fee for a job and will enjoy working on it, it doesn't matter if no one will ever see it.
- Pleasure – if you'll enjoy working on a project and will get some great promotion opportunities from it, you can afford to do it at a reduced price.
- Promotion – if you'll get great promotional opportunities from a project and will be paid really well, it might be worth doing even if you won't enjoy the work that much.

Your personal pricing guide

Your first step *always* is to ask the client what their budget is: this is essential data-gathering. As mentioned previously, you might not necessarily get an answer – but if you do, it will make things much easier.

Editorial

Editorial includes magazines, newspapers and online articles. Magazines, for example, know exactly how much they want to spend on illustration for a page or feature – they do it regularly – and most of the time they'll tell you.

Over time, you'll get to know which kinds of magazines pay what, and what the price difference should be between a cover and a full-page, half-page or quarter-page. When you accumulate and record this data over time, it becomes your personal guide of what's expected and reasonable, and what's too low or too high. The more data you have, the easier assessing price becomes.

What are they willing to pay?

Charlie is an art director. They've been given a budget for a feature that requires illustration: they might tell you what it is, but probably won't tell you the maximum budget. If there's £500 to spend, Charlie might say it's £400; they'll reserve that 20% in case any extra revisions need to be made and paid for, and assume some illustrators will negotiate on their initial price.

In the same way that we might quote £900 for a project, we'd probably do it for £800 – it's a two-way street. The client has a number they *want* to pay, and a number they're *willing* to pay.

One clue to a magazine's budget is its circulation (i.e. how many copies it produces each issue) and what the subject is. For example, a gardening magazine typically will be less well funded than a glossy lifestyle magazine filled with adverts for high-value products such as watches, designer clothing and fragrances. There are always exceptions, but you can tell a lot about a magazine from the readers it's trying to attract.

Magazine projects are relatively easy to get to grips with because the way they use illustration is straightforward: they appear in the printed magazine for a limited time, and may accompany the same article online. There are plenty of good reasons for an illustrator to start their career in editorial, as it's a quick way to learn the ropes and a useful proving ground.

Branding and advertising

The problem arrives when an illustrator is asked to give a price for a more complicated project with multiple territories, a variety of uses and use of the work for longer periods of time – which is common in the higher-paying parts of the industry such as branding or advertising.

Clients who bring projects like this to you are less likely to reveal their budget: they might not know yet how much they can spend, if they're still scoping out the possibilities for the project. If they do know their budget, they might tell you – so always ask, just in case. But if they don't, they could be looking around for the right price/value trade-off.

More complicated and higher-budget projects are less likely to be offered to a beginner, so as a new illustrator you're less likely to be put in a position where you have to give a price with no experience. If you are, membership to the Association of Illustrators (see the Further resources) can be incredibly valuable: the Association might not give you exact prices for the reasons outlined above, but it can guide you to submitting a fair price for your circumstances.

You also could ask a more experienced illustrator for help, but the price they submit is likely to be higher than yours, precisely because they are more experienced. If you're lucky enough to work with other illustrators in a studio or have friends in a similar position to you, share what you discover about budgets from different clients with each other. Having your own data is useful, but shared data from a group of illustrators means you'll get to know what realistic upper and lower limits are for different kinds of projects much quicker.

Low price equals low value

Out of fear of quoting too high and losing a job, many new illustrators quote far too low instead: they think that giving a lower price will increase their chances of a client taking a punt on them. This may work in some cases, but as we saw in Chapter 9, a client won by the lowest price isn't necessarily one with long-term value: as soon as we grow in confidence and put our prices up, they won't want to work with us any more (which isn't necessarily a bad thing).

There will be an endless supply of people willing to do the job cheaper than you – so giving the lowest quote you can in the hope of securing more projects, means you're setting yourself up for a very difficult life by competing to be the lowest-priced option.

Presenting a very low price to a client who regularly deals with professional illustrators sets the tone for the whole relationship: if we don't see ourselves as someone who makes work worth paying good money for, why should the client? When we give our lowest possible price, the client might perceive that our work is low quality and low value – and that's difficult to change when we want to raise our price in the future. For example, if the client works with us a few times on projects around the £300 level, they might not consider us the right person for the job when they've got a project with a £5,000 budget.

Raising your prices will lose you some clients, and that's okay. You'll do that multiple times over your career as you start to work with bigger and better clients. Clients with unrealistically low budgets, who only care about price, are almost always the ones that complain the most – and make unreasonable demands.

Price appropriately to your level

Some new illustrators who have learned a bit about how to price their work will present a figure to the client that's reasonable for a professional. But as we discovered above, beginners can't necessarily charge the same for services as a seasoned pro, who can command higher fees because they:

- Have more experience
- Can offer more value
- Have proof that they're worth that price – in the form of their portfolio full of client work.

As we saw in Chapter 11, illustrators who can offer a client more value can charge more, in the same way that professional singers, footballers or carpenters have a higher price than amateurs.

A beginner with very little experience or social proof has low value to a client, and that client has endless options if they're willing to work with new industry entrants. There's no reason for them to pay professional rates for an inexperienced illustrator, because they could simply work with an experienced professional instead. This doesn't necessarily mean those clients want to work with the very cheapest option (because a really cheap illustrator may be low quality), but they do want good value for money.

Aim for the ballpark

When a client receives a range of quotes, usually they won't go for the most expensive or the cheapest; they'll pick from the middle, because it's a good trade-off between price and perceived quality.

The price we give to a client is affected by the range of other quotes they've received: the highest will always seem too high, and the lowest suggests they won't receive good work in return. If a client is choosing from a range of unknown, inexperienced illustrators, they'll select from somewhere in-between.

You'll get a better sense of what reasonable prices are as time goes on: you just have to be in the right ballpark to be seriously considered – that's all you really need. The Graphic Artists Guild[30] publishes a useful book with guide price ranges for different industries in the US market; naturally it can't be accurate for every client you'll encounter, but it can give you an approximation to aim for when you do quote.

When you're pricing, sometimes you can afford to be a little bit too high, because the client can negotiate with you (more on this below). If it's a bit low, sure – you're leaving money on the table, but you're not representing yourself as a low-quality option. You'll still be taken seriously!

If you can figure out the right ballpark, then you can make your best guess.

Value versus cost

When we buy a product, the value we get from it has to outweigh the price we've paid, otherwise it's not a good trade. This book focuses so heavily on new illustrators improving their skills, partly because the more you develop and the more value you can offer, the more you can charge for your work.

Although calculating an hourly or daily rate is a useful rule-of-thumb when you don't have much data to help with pricing, it doesn't factor in what the work is worth to the client – or indeed any specific details about the project. An hourly rate is about you and what you want or need to make to survive, but you're not only charging the client for your time.

What it costs you to create the work is largely irrelevant; pricing for value is about the benefit the client is gaining from the illustrations you

---

30   Graphic Artists Guild (2021) *The Graphic Artists Guild Handbook: Pricing & Ethical Guidelines*, 16th edition, MIT Press. Available at: https://graphicartistsguild.org/the-graphic-artists-guild-handbook-pricing-ethical-guidelines/

provide. For example, if you're working on an internal company project that few people are likely to see, it's low value: you can't charge much for that kind of project. But if your illustrations are going to be used to make the client a lot of money by attracting new customers, helping to sell a high-value product or redefining their brand, those are high-value projects and should be charged at a high price.

What value is the client getting?

Say you're working on the packaging for a chocolate bar for a small independent company: that packaging might help them make £10,000 in profit over the course of a year. However, that same work applied to the product of one of the largest chocolate brands in the world could help make that company 50x that amount.

In that case your work is providing more value to the bigger client, so they're (usually) willing to pay more.

As we've seen, average work has low value, and a client has plenty of alternatives if that's what they want – in this kind of situation, they won't pay high prices because they don't need to. But if you have well-developed creative skills that few others possess – and if you think in a way that few other illustrators can – you can charge a lot more.

Clients and consumers don't think about the specific prices they paid long-term as much as the value they got from a purchase, good or bad. If you deliver something low value to a client they'll remember it, but they'll also remember if you deliver exceptional quality and value to their project.

What kind of client is it?

The size and kind of client is a factor in how we price work. Generally, large multinational corporations have higher budgets than smaller independents. This can complicate things when providing a quote, because what we charge a large client won't necessarily be the same as what we'd charge a small client for the same kind of work.

Some might consider this pricing discrimination – the price should be the price, period – but when thinking about value pricing, the work done for a large international company has a much greater potential impact. In addition, as we've already discovered, better clients want to work with higher-calibre creatives, so they expect to pay more for an elevated service. That small independent company probably couldn't afford to work with the best creative talent, so they work with less experienced and lower-priced illustrators instead.

Of course, everything we deliver to a client – no matter what the budget – should be high quality; but what we deliver to a client with £20,000 to spend will be quite different to what we deliver to one with £500. The amount of time we spend, and the solutions we offer to a higher-paying client, should be a lot more. They're paying a premium price for a premium service and a £20,000 client is more valuable, so we put in more effort and offer them something really special.

Negotiating

Appear confident in your price

It may take a while before you *become* confident in how you price your work, but whenever you do give a quote to a client, *appear* confident in what you're proposing. If the client senses you're unsure about your price, you're inviting them to pay less than you're worth. Their job is to get the most work out of a freelancer for the lowest cost: if they can see you're uncertain, they might come back by pushing the figure much lower, knowing you'll probably accept it. If you inadvertently communicate to the client that you don't know your own value, they'll decide it for you.

However unconfident you might be feeling about the quotes you send, do keep it to yourself. If you're sure of your price and offer, that doesn't mean the client won't try to negotiate – but they'll be discussing it with a professional, rather than with someone of whom they can take advantage.

There are certain things illustrators need to know to be able to give an accurate price. Asking questions about the project and how the work will be used doesn't convey lack of confidence – in fact, it's quite the opposite. If we're asking the right questions, the client assumes we know what we're talking about and that we're calculating our price accordingly.

Asking no questions marks us out as an amateur and invites lowball offers.

Practise negotiating early

Most new illustrators are too scared to negotiate, and it's no surprise. If we're on the cusp of securing a paying client, why rock the boat and risk losing them?

Two reasons:

- This is your livelihood – you're doing it to make money, so if you can make 25% more from a project, that's a big deal.
- Clients expect it – while it's personal (and possibly emotional) for you, it's not for the client. The art director isn't spending their own money!

You won't always feel like it's necessary to negotiate the price a client offers: if you get one that's above what you would have quoted, you're already winning – but it's a good idea to practise negotiating early, while the stakes are low.

For example, if you're offered £400, try asking the client if they can stretch to £480. It's an insignificant amount for them and unlikely to lose you the project, but it's a 20% pay rise for you. If they say 'No', so be it: but you've practised asking and are developing your skills and confidence – and they might say 'Yes' or offer you something in-between. Either way, you're winning!

Look forward to negotiating

If you've been asked to give the client a quote for a project and appeared confident in that, hopefully the client will start to negotiate with you. If they don't, that probably means you didn't quote high enough. Ideally, the price should be high enough to get the client to start negotiating: you can always reduce your price, but if it's too low you can't ask for more once you've made an offer.

If they do start to negotiate, it means they're seriously interested in working with you. It's a positive sign so you can negotiate confidently, knowing you're in the right ballpark. Don't fear negotiation, look forward to it!

With each back-and-forth while you're negotiating, the goal isn't to win; rather, to keep the conversation going until you both land on an agreeable solution – then you both win. If your price is way too high straight off the bat, the conversation ends. If the client makes you an unreasonably low offer, the conversation also ends (or you end up doing the work anyway, feeling undervalued the whole time).

Negotiate on deliverables before cost

If the client wants you to lower your price, first consider the project and what's required of you. If their budget is, say, 20% less than your quote, ask them if there are any non-essential deliverables that could be removed.

This won't be applicable if you're just working on one illustration. But for example, if you're working on a larger set, including:

- 1 x hero/header illustration
- 5 x banner illustrations
- 4 x spot illustrations
- 8 x icons

– some are more likely to be important to the client than others. Do they really need five banners, or would they be happy with three?

You gave your price for a reason: your confidently presented quote wasn't plucked out of thin air, after all! To drop it as soon as they ask shows that the price was arbitrary. If they want to pay 20% less, they should be willing to negotiate on deliverables. If they can be flexible, you can too.

If you drop your price by 10% and they can cut down on what you need to deliver, you can find a happy middle ground together.

There's always time to think about your price

As a new illustrator, you'll be negotiating with people who are more experienced at it: they do it on a regular basis, so it comes easily. They also know they have the upper hand if you're an entrant to the industry and still finding your feet.

Always take the time to consider your quotes and responses carefully. If you're invited onto a call with a client and they ask for a price, you might feel you need to give an answer right there and then, or risk losing the job. They know that, it's exactly why they've put you on the spot: they want you to make a snap decision without considering all the options. Inevitably, you'll come to regret it if rushing to give an answer, because you haven't done the maths or really thought about it.

The client doesn't need an answer immediately: they might need it quickly, but there's always time for you to go away and think about it. It's fine to say you'll get back to them in the next couple of hours; this way, you can give a more considered quote as a result. They won't hold it against you – and if they do, they're revealing themselves as a client who is trying to take advantage and should be avoided.

The unobtainable triangle

A model which can be helpful when setting and negotiating a price

for a project is the 'unobtainable triangle':

- If a client needs the work done quickly and cheaply, they can't expect high quality.
- If a client wants high quality quickly, they can't expect it to be cheap.
- If a client wants high quality for a low price, they can't get it quickly.

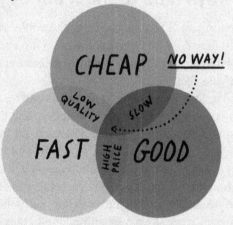

It's considered unobtainable because if a company or service provider are providing all three at the same time, their business model is flawed. An illustrator would need to work to a high quality incredibly quickly and charge peanuts for it!

They couldn't last: they'd either go out of business or burn themselves out, trying to do all three.

Offer high value and charge a high price

When we're looking to negotiate a significantly higher price, or the client tells us that our quote is higher than the others they've received, we need to be offering much higher value to justify it.

If you're the best fit for the project due to your specialist skills or style, you can be the highest quote and still win it. If you know you're the best choice for the client, the task here isn't to lower the price, but to communicate to them why it's higher and you're worth it.

Sell the benefits of working with you, and tell them what exceptional service they can expect by:

- Talking about your process and how you develop your ideas
- Telling them why you're a good fit for their brand
- Offering multiple concepts for them to review
- Telling them why you appreciate collaborating with great art directors, and how together you'll make this project the very best it can be.

Only the highest-performing creative talent goes this far. When you can make a client see how much value you'll add to their project and show them how you'll meet their needs, they'll be happy to pay a high price.

Next, we're going to take a look at what you need to know about the legals: copyright, confidentiality, licensing and contracts.

Key takeaways

- Experiment with pricing and accumulate data.
- Ask what the client's budget is, every time.
- A low price can give the impression that your work has low value.
- Work out the production cost – how many hours you need to do the job.
- Your price only needs to be in the right ballpark to be seriously considered.
- Consider the value that the client is getting from your work.
- Be confident in the prices you give.
- Practise negotiating before the stakes are high.
- Negotiate on deliverables as well as price.
- Don't rush into giving a price without considering it carefully.
- If you can offer exceptional work, you can charge a high price.

14

Licensing, rights and contracts

Non-disclosure agreements

We touched on non-disclosure agreements (NDAs) in Chapter 9; they're also called 'confidentiality agreements'. These are documents you'll receive from clients – usually bigger companies – who want to know you'll keep a project confidential until its release date. These clients might be releasing a new product or service which they understandably want to keep under wraps until the big launch. Everyone working on the project will be required to sign one of these documents to guarantee its secrecy.

Generally speaking, no matter what the project is and whether you receive an NDA or not, it's best to consider any project confidential until the client makes it public – and to let the client know you will treat it as such. This reassures them that you're a professional.

NDAs are common – and if an illustrator treats each project confidentially anyway, they're nothing to worry about. However, if an artist has signed an NDA then posts a project online before its official release date, there is a legal paper trail – they might be required to pay damages to the client for breach of confidentiality. Sometimes a figure is specified in the NDA – £10,000 is common – which is high enough to make anyone think twice about revealing anything about a project prior to its going live.

The client sends the illustrator an NDA before they can release any details of the project. By signing it, you aren't obliged to complete the commission, or even take it on – but you won't be able to find out any more about it until you do. If a client does ask you for a quote before revealing the details of the brief, you can't give an accurate price. Where they aren't forthcoming with details, you might need to ask them if they need you to sign an NDA to be able to give them a well-considered quote.

There is one thing to look out for in NDAs: sometimes they include as standard terms that assign to the client the rights to any work you produce for them. This is a sneaky tactic, as terms of this nature have no place in a confidentiality agreement. It means you would be agreeing to hand over your intellectual property (IP) before even knowing what the project is.

Unfair NDA clauses to watch for

Here's an example of the kind of text that might indicate this. It's usually to be found under an 'Intellectual Property' heading:

> All copyright, design rights, trademarks, patent rights and similar rights whether registered or not ('IP Rights') in the Information shall belong to and vest in [client] or its licensors.
> You agree that you will not obtain or claim rights in the Information and *will assign to us (with full title guarantee and including by way of present assignment of future copyright) all IP Rights in any works you produce based on or using the Information.*
> You also waive any moral rights therein and agree and acknowledge that we may use, modify and adapt the works in any way we see fit.

The first part of this extract states that the information the client provides is their IP – and remains so. That's fair: the illustrator doesn't own the information that the client sends to them.

The second part (in italic) is not fair. It states that anything the illustrator produces for the client after signing the NDA automatically belongs to them: this is known as a 'rights grab', and is unreasonable in this kind of document.

Additionally, by signing this document, the illustrator waives their moral rights (more on this later in this chapter) which, among other things, means they won't even be credited as the creator of the illustrations; the client could even have another illustrator make changes to the original illustrator's work.

In these NDAs the wording will vary and can be confusing. It's fine to accept that the information the client provides remains their property, but do not accept your rights being assigned to the client at this stage. (We'll look at selling the rights to your work later in this chapter.)

Should you come across these unfair terms in an NDA, simply quote the unreasonable wording and email it back to the client, along with a note saying:

> I'm afraid I can't agree to assigning my rights in an NDA before knowing the details of the project. I'm happy to discuss it later if necessary but for now, can we remove it? Then I'll be happy to sign. I'm looking forward to hearing more about the project.

This is a perfectly reasonable request. If the client refuses, unfortunately it's a signal that they're trying to take advantage of you.

Licensing your work

If we've calculated what a reasonable hourly or daily rate would be, we have a baseline to build on: we know our minimum to charge to survive, if we trade an hour of time for money – this is our production cost. But there are a lot of additional factors to consider when pricing for value.

Musicians, photographers, architects, playwrights and many other creative professionals license their work for specific purposes – and illustration is no different. We give a client permission to use our illustrations for a specific project in return for a fee, and calculate the licence fee based on how the illustration will be used. When the licence runs out, the client must stop using it or must ask to extend it for an additional fee. Once a licence expires on that illustration, as the copyright holder you are free to license it to another client, if you wish.

As a general rule-of-thumb, the more people that will see the final product, the higher the price should be. For example:

- Generally, a weekly magazine pays less than a monthly magazine because it's in circulation for less time.
- Packaging for a small independent coffee roaster would pay less than a brand found in a national supermarket.

- An advertising campaign shown for one week in one city pays less than an international campaign running for three months.

There are exceptions: some weekly magazines have a much larger readership than many monthlies; and for advertising it depends on who the client is, what the product is and the location of the campaign. For example, an advert displayed in New York's Times Square for a few days would be seen by far more people than a three-month campaign running in rural England. As a general guideline, thinking about how many people will see the work is a good starting point.

What makes a licence?

The specific licence the client requires is likely to include a few variables, so to provide an accurate quote you need to know about:

- Usage
- Territory
- Duration.

Usage

This is how the work will be used. It could be in print, digital, social media, outdoor advertising, packaging or any number of other ways, and for one specific purpose or a combination of different uses. The licence might be 'all media', which means it could be used for anything.

Territory

This is where the work will be used. For example, it could be as small as one location for the opening of a new store, or in stores all over the world. It might be for one country or a whole continent.

Duration

This is how long the work will be used. For a store opening, the work might be used only for a week or 'in perpetuity' – which means the client can use it forever, if they wish. Some projects are shown for days, others for years.

Sometimes the client won't know how long they want to use the work for, so you could offer some different options, for example: one, three or five years. The price quoted is calculated based on the above factors, so if the client changes any of them, the price changes accordingly.

Licence examples

Here are two examples of how a licence could be written: a simple one and a more complex one.

Licence A

Usage: Editorial (printed magazine and associated online article)*
Territory: United Kingdom
Duration: 90 days[†]

Licence B

Usage: Out-of-home advertising (OOH),[‡] print, digital, social media and marketing
Territory: Austria, Germany, Switzerland
Duration: 5 years

In these two examples, the amount of time spent making the illustration might be the same, but the client is getting far more use and value from Licence B: it's used for lots of different things, in several countries and for a long time.

The price for Licence B should be considerably higher.

---

[*] An online article is likely to live online forever in an archive of the magazine's articles. This is normal and accepted.
[†] A monthly magazine usually requires about 90 days' exclusivity for the illustration. They don't want an illustrator to relicense the image to another magazine too quickly; this is also normal and accepted.
[‡] Billboards, posters, etc.

Copyright basics

When you produce an illustration or any other creative work, you own it – it is your IP. This means you, the creator, are the only one who has the right to copy it. When a magazine publishes your illustration, they have paid for the *usage of a copy of your work* on their page. You give the client permission to use your IP in return for a fee.

As we saw in Chapter 6, copying is a useful way to develop our skills – but if we then try to sell that imitation of another artist's work, we're infringing their copyright. The original creator is the only person with the right to do that. Being influenced by other artists in our professional work is expected and unavoidable; but if we try to pass off someone else's creation as our own, not only are we infringing another artist's rights, we're doing ourselves an active disservice by not aiming for originality. Similarly, if someone copies one of our own illustrations or uses it without our permission, they're infringing our rights too.

Most people aren't familiar with copyright law: they often assume that any image they find on the internet is fair game. It can be infuriating for creatives to see their work copied or stolen; but rather than responding in anger, take a step back and consider that the offender is simply unaware they're doing anything wrong. Don't assume malice when ignorance is a more likely explanation.[31]

---

31   'Hanlon's Razor' reminds us that not everyone is actively out to get us, they just may not realise they're doing it. Model Thinkers (2023) 'Hanlon's Razor'. Available at: https://modelthinkers. com/mental-model/hanlons-razor

How to handle breach of copyright

Write an email to the person or company using or copying your work, and explain the situation:

1. Tell them that you are the copyright holder and creator of the illustration.
2. Point out that you haven't given them permission to use it.
3. Depending on the situation, ask that the work be taken down or credited to you properly. For example, if there is a benefit to having your work on a certain website and you're fully credited, that could be a good thing. If it's a low-quality site and you don't want your work associated with it, ask for it to be removed.
4. If the work is being used commercially by a brand, you're well within your rights to ask for compensation and charge a fee for it.

Don't issue threats: just consider this first contact friendly advice to someone potentially unaware of their mistake. Sometimes it is an innocent error, and sometimes it isn't – but it's best to begin with a friendly tone. Most of the time this is enough for the work to be removed: the offender either might respond apologetically, presumably because they're embarrassed about their blunder; or not at all, because they've been caught red-handed in trying to rip you off.

If this doesn't work, consider asking a legal professional to issue an official 'cease and desist' letter.

Fair dealing

There are instances when an illustrator's work can be reproduced without permission or payment, known as 'fair dealing' or 'fair use'. In most cases, the illustrator should still be credited.

- Research and study – this is allowed if there is no commercial purpose. For example, including other illustrators' work in college coursework.
- News reporting – a creative work can be shown in

journalism. No doubt you'll have seen photos on the news with a credit to the photographer.

- Criticism or reviews – if a magazine reviews a public gallery show, it can reproduce artwork relating to the show, if it credits the artist(s) – the review is considered publicity for the work.
- Incidental inclusion – for example, a holiday photo of family with an advertising billboard in the background.
- Parody – this is a tricky one, but something you're unlikely to encounter as an illustrator unless you want to work in satirical cartoons. A parody of an artistic work, often for comedic purposes, is allowed because it's a right to freedom of speech. However, the work must still respect the copyright holder's rights. If it could do potential harm to the copyright holder, that's where it can get into trouble. (This is why, for example, the musician 'Weird Al' Yankovic always asks permission before he parodies a song, because often they're making fun of the song or its artist.)

Selling the rights to your work

Sometimes, a client will want to buy the rights to your work so that the copyright is assigned to them. Once they own it, you no longer have any right to use it yourself or any say in how it's used. They can use the work forever, for whatever they want –and they don't have to give you any credit for it.

These kinds of deals should be considered very carefully. The price you quote for assigning your rights should factor in all possible uses of the work by the client, and be appropriately higher than a licensed option.

There is no one-size-fits-all rule for calculating this kind of quote, as it requires each illustrator to consider the possible trade-off in short-term gain versus long-term value: this will be different for everyone, depending on their circumstances.

Usually, somewhere between 2x and 3x the rate is about right; but if you're trying to calculate a buyout price, consider the illustration's long-term usefulness to you. If it's of a very specific niche subject, you might not be able to relicense it to any other client in the future anyway

– in which case, getting a slightly higher price for it in the short term could be a good idea. If the illustration seems like it could be useful and valuable to other kinds of clients, you might regret selling the rights to it.

Contract essentials

Contracts protect you, perhaps even more so than the client that sends it to you. As a freelancer you have less money and power, and you don't have a legal department – while a £5,000 project is a big deal for you, it might not be for your client.

If the agreement between you and your client isn't set out clearly in writing, all kinds of practical and legal difficulties can arise, should things go sideways. If there's an imbalance of power and resources, a big client could steamroller you into submission.

You don't need to be a legal professional to understand a contract, but it takes some work to become familiar with them – especially when their language can seem intentionally confusing.

Never sign a contract that you don't understand.

It's not uncommon to establish a trusting and friendly relationship with an art director, then receive a contract from their company's legal department that's completely at odds with the values you've witnessed in the creative department. Most contracts you'll receive as a freelance illustrator won't be trying to trick you, but often there will be clauses that aren't in your favour and that you'll want to change. If you know what you're looking for and what is reasonable, you can ask for amendments with confidence – or walk away, if the contract is genuinely unreasonable and can't be changed.

Reading through contracts with a fine-tooth comb is a laborious and challenging task, so asking for advice is worthwhile. While you won't need to enlist a lawyer for every contract you receive, you may want to speak to one to help you learn what to look out for. Also, you can seek advice from people who are familiar with freelance contracts, such as agents or a contract adviser from the Association of Illustrators.

What makes a contract?

As a brief introduction, there are five essential parts of a contract:

1. Offer – the client asks the illustrator to do something for them.
2. Acceptance – the illustrator agrees to take on the project, perhaps by signing an agreement or sending a confirmation email.
3. Consideration – what the illustrator receives in return for their contribution (usually money).
4. Certainty of terms – a description of the project, key dates, licence details, the illustrator's details, the client's details, payment structure, etc. Most disputes arise because contracts are insufficiently clear, but a contract can still be made even if key issues have not been properly defined.
5. Intention to enter legal relations – both parties must intend for the proposed agreement to be legally binding.

All of the necessary elements of a contract might be in a written agreement, but they can also arise through verbal exchange, email, SMS (or other forms of instant messaging), or a combination of these.

It's always advisable to get the contractual details of a project written and sent by email before starting work: this leaves a clear paper trail of what's been discussed and agreed, which you can refer back to easily. Verbal confirmation is difficult to prove if you should find yourself in a disagreement, so if you do agree anything on the phone or in person, be sure to write it down and email it to the client to confirm everything is in order.

Beginning work on a project can be interpreted as acceptance of the client's terms – but if you encounter a problem, the client could deny that they gave you the go-ahead. It's much safer to have everything settled in writing, and *only begin the work once both parties are in agreement.*

If the necessary details are stated in an email from your client and you agree by email, you have entered into a contract.

Other clauses to look out for

Copyright or intellectual property

Be sure to check this section carefully to ensure you aren't accidentally handing over your rights to the client.

Confidentiality

This will be important to your client and appear in most contracts. But as we've already covered, even if it doesn't, be mindful that sharing your illustrations before your paying client does isn't allowed.

Non-compete clause

Often this can be overlooked, but a 'restriction of business' clause might mean you aren't able to work on similar-themed illustrations or projects with similar clients in future, which could be severely limiting to you (more on this below). By agreeing to a contract with this clause in it, you can easily slash your opportunities for future work.

For example, if you work on a financial-themed illustration and sign a contract that says you can't work on a similar subject, that's a huge area in which you're no longer permitted to do business. Or if you work on a children's book and sign an unreasonable non-compete clause, that's it – no more children's books!

Always request that this clause be removed, as it restricts your opportunities to find other work as a freelancer. If it can't be removed, it should be made as detailed and specific as possible.

Don't restrict your future opportunities

I work with an illustrator who works on a lot of children's books. We received a non-compete clause in a contract for a dinosaur-themed book (there are a lot of dinosaur-themed opportunities in children's publishing!) The publisher refused to remove the clause entirely, but we were able to make it so specific to the particular project that it wouldn't restrict the illustrator in the future.

> Instead of not being able to work on any further dinosaur books at all, the artist was only restricted in working on dinosaur-themed, ABC pop-up books for five-to-seven-year-olds. Since then, they've been able to work on several other dinosaur-related books for kids.

Moral rights

These give you the right to be identified as the work's creator. If you were to waive these rights, the client is under no obligation to credit you for it. Moral rights also give you the right to object to derogatory treatment of your work, if the client were to decide to get another designer to make changes to your illustration, for example.

Cancellation and rejection terms

These are important because your project could be cancelled for any number of reasons, whether by you or the client. You want to make sure you get paid for the work you've done, if it is cancelled. Equally, if your work is rejected, you still need to be paid for the time you spent on it.

The Association of Illustrators has some recommended guidelines for 'kill fees'.[32] A kill fee is a payment structure for cancellation agreed with the client before a project starts:

- 25% of the agreed fee if cancelled before the roughs are delivered
- 33% of the agreed fee at the amend stage
- 100% of the agreed fee when the work is complete.

Additionally, if the job is cancelled, it should be made clear that the rights in the illustrations stay with you.

'Entire agreement' clause

Many contracts have this clause: it means that the contract constitutes the only enforceable agreement. It supersedes whatever may have been

---

32   Association of Illustrators (2020) 'Cancellation/kill fees and coronavirus'. Available at: https://theaoi.com/2020/03/12/cancellation-kill-fees-and-coronavirus

previously agreed by email or over the phone – so you need to make sure the contract accurately reflects what you have discussed with your client.

There are many more clauses in a typical contract beyond the scope of this book – this is just an outline of the essential parts. The Illustrator's Guide to Law and Legal Practice[33] published by the Association of Illustrators is fantastic resource for a more in-depth look at contracts and more.

Insurance

Some of the bigger clients won't consider working with an illustrator who doesn't have professional indemnity insurance. This type of insurance covers an act, error or omission in the course of work that causes financial loss to a client.

For example, if we were to accidentally use a reference photograph in our work that belongs to a photographer, and that photographer takes legal action against our client – if we've signed a contract, in all likelihood we as the illustrator would be responsible for those losses.

While these situations are rare, it could happen – so just for peace of mind, you might want to consider investing in insurance. Not only does it protect you, should something bad happen, but it can give the bigger clients more confidence in working with you.

Get it in writing

Often an illustrator finds themselves in a position where they're working with a client who doesn't have a contract – and perhaps understands them less than they do. In this case, it's important to be able to construct a legally enforceable agreement to send to the client.

---

33   Simon Stern (2008) *The illustrator's Guide to Law and Legal Practice*, Association of Illustrators. Available at: https://theaoi.com/product/illustrators-guide-to-law-and-business-practice-digital-version/

The Association of Illustrators offers a downloadable commissioning agreement template[34] for members, which I recommend using. It gives space to fill in the necessary details about the project, as well as general terms and conditions including kill fees, payment terms, ownership of copyright and more. This can be sent to the client to sign before beginning work.

Getting everything in writing – and having the client agree to it in writing – becomes the proof that both of you have entered into a legal agreement, if things should go badly. In most cases, taking legal action against a client isn't a realistic option for a freelancer: it's expensive and unless a large sum is owed, it's probably not worth the time it would take to resolve.

When a client receives a contract from you that outlines exactly how they can and can't use your work, and states how much they have to pay you for it, hopefully it should stop them from doing something stupid like taking your work and not paying you. If they're unwilling to sign a contract, it's a red flag and that client should be avoided.

In the next chapter we'll look at agents: what they do, whether you need one and how to get one.

Key takeaways

- Look out for unfavourable terms in NDA documents.
- Find out what licence the client needs (usage, territory, duration).
- Never sign a contract you don't understand.
- Only assign your copyright if the price is right.
- Agree cancellation and kill fees.
- Don't allow a contract to restrict your future opportunities.
- Consider getting professional indemnity insurance.
- Use the Association of Illustrators' commissioning agreement form for clients who don't send a contract.
- Get essential project details in writing, so you can refer to them easily.

---

34   Association of Illustrators (n.d.) 'Illustrator commissioner agreement'. Available at: https://theaoi.com/resources/contracts/illustrator-commissioner-agreement

15

Finding an agent

The benefits of working with an agent

For a creative career to thrive, not only does an artist need exceptional creative skills, they also need to be able to sell those skills to clients: without both, making a living is impossible. These skills can be learned, but many illustrators choose to outsource the selling part to an agent so they can concentrate on what they enjoy the most.

Not every illustrator needs or wants an agent, and not everyone wants to pay for one. An agent offers a service to illustrators, partly providing skills and resources that some illustrators may not have fully developed yet such as business experience, negotiation skills, legal know-how and pricing knowledge.

Business experience

This can cover everything from sales and marketing to finance and project management. Many creatives prefer to focus on the aspects they enjoy, and leave the admin and paperwork to someone better suited or more interested in handling it.

Negotiation

Anyone can acquire and practise this skill, but it can be intimidating for an inexperienced freelancer. After all, as we've seen, the clients we negotiate with do it on a regular basis. An agent can level the playing field in this area because they're experienced negotiators.

Legal knowledge

Agents aren't lawyers, but they read a lot of contracts and know what to look out for in them. Also, they can determine what's reasonable or unreasonable in a contract. Many illustrators find it a huge relief to have an agent handle contracts for them.

Pricing knowledge

As discussed in Chapter 13, this comes with experience: illustrators generally get better at it over time. However, an agent might work on the same volume of projects in a month as a freelancer does in a year. This allows them to discover acceptable prices much faster: they see a range of pricing possibilities from clients every day, from insultingly low to surprisingly high, giving them a good sense of the market.

A good agent can help an illustrator reach career heights they might not be able to on their own, and can introduce them to lots of different kinds of projects. An established agency has a wide network of connections with clients that would take an individual illustrator years to build.

Artists with agents are perceived as being at a certain professional standard by clients. A client may see an individual freelancer with little experience as a risk – but if they have an agent, the client is more likely to trust in their abilities and professionalism. This is because the illustrator has already been 'chosen' by the agency, providing social proof and a mark of quality.

Additionally, artists represented by agents have a support network and help available to them if they need it, reducing the likelihood of encountering a problem that can't be solved.

What an agent can do for you

Here are a few of the things an agent can do for an illustrator's career:

- Advise on it – whether a regular portfolio review or broader career advice.
- Handle the minutiae, so you don't have to – agents can deal with some of the less enjoyable aspects of your work, so you can focus on what you love.

- List you on their website – simply appearing on an agency's website or promotions means immediately more eyes on your work.
- Know your work's worth – agents work on a lot of projects.
- Give good price advice – agents have a good idea of what different kinds of clients will pay for various types of work. This experience takes a lot of the guesswork out of pricing. It's easier for an agent to negotiate prices when there is less personal and emotional connection to the work.
- Advise on contracts – agents know what is reasonable and unreasonable in a contract, and can protect you from unfavourable terms.
- Offer a clear-eyed view – they see the work more objectively and can sell it without fear of failure or impostor syndrome.
- Address issues with clients – if you have a problem with a client, part of the agent's role is to solve it: you can avoid difficult conversations by asking your agent for help. An agent can play 'bad cop' and lay down the law with a troublesome client, so you don't have to.
- Offer experienced marketing advice – having an agent means help from people who are seasoned in marketing work. They will show your work and can help you improve the ways you show it.
- Discuss your work knowledgeably – often, agents have a creative background, so they can talk to you about your work with at least some knowledge of your technical process.
- Give good client insight – agents know which clients are good to work with and which aren't.
- Fight for your rights – if you've been treated unfairly by a client or your work has been used without authorisation (or payment).

What an agent can't do

An agent can't:

- Sell bad work to the best clients
- Fill your schedule with incredible projects 100% of the time
- Change your career fast
- Make clients like your style
- Decide what you want for your career.

It's also worth mentioning that getting an agent isn't going to make you rich and famous overnight! They'll promote you to the best of their ability – but if you aren't making new work regularly, they won't have anything to promote.

What does an agency look for?

Each agency wants specific qualities in an illustrator, depending on the kinds of talent they already represent. Some general areas that an agency assesses a new applicant on are:

- Style
- Technical skills
- Professionalism
- Honesty
- Personality and attitude
- A team player.

Let's look at each one in turn.

Style

An artist's style is key for illustration agencies: they need to see that your work is commercially viable and will appeal to their clients. They want artists with unique, recognisable styles who their clients will ask for by name and line up to work with – these are the artists who get asked to work on big, high-profile projects and can command higher fees.

Technical skills

The agency will be looking at your technical skills: if your work doesn't meet the minimum standards for professional illustration (which we'll look at later in this chapter), it won't be considered. Be sure to present your illustrations professionally because if they aren't, it doesn't matter how good the content is. It's key to show that you can deliver work that meets those specifications.

Professionalism

Agents need to know they can trust an illustrator if they're going to recommend them to their clients. They want to work with someone whose work is consistent, who communicates clearly, manages their time well and delivers what they promise.

When you apply to an agency, your portfolio and how you communicate with them (through email, for example), are all they have to go on. While the illustration world is informal, it's important to be considerate, concise and clear in your communication. Professionals aren't perfect – you're not expected to be! – but they can admit faults, take ownership of mistakes and communicate any potential problems that could affect their work.

Honesty

Agents know that new artists just starting out don't have the same skills and experience as seasoned professionals yet, so it's part of their role to help them develop.

To secure an agent, it isn't necessary to pretend we have skills that we really don't yet. If we're open about where we are now and what we want to achieve, the agent can help us grow our career; but if we're not completely honest about why we can't do something or meet a deadline, it can waste their time.

Being upfront about problems means they can help us solve them more effectively.

Personality and attitude

Being friends isn't necessary for a productive professional relationship, but a friendly relationship does make things easier. For an agent to take on a self-centred diva, that illustrator's work needs to have enormous commercial potential. An agency might put up with that kind of behaviour for a while if clients are lining up to work with the artist, but it won't last. If an artist isn't pleasant to work with, eventually nobody will want to commission them!

Conversely, an illustrator who is proactive, enthusiastic, open to feedback and friendly has a much better chance of working with great clients in the long term.

A team player

An agent needs an illustrator to work with them towards the same goal, a team player: someone who wants their agency and its other artists to succeed. If the other artists within the agency become popular, its profile is raised along with all of its artists. Showing support and encouraging colleagues demonstrates that we're part of the team.

Consider what you can offer to the agency and your fellow illustrators, and you'll become an important part of that collective. You'll be the artist your agent recommends more often because of your terrific attitude: they'll trust you to deliver great work to their most important clients, and your teammates will want you to succeed because you've shown you're rooting for them too.

An artist who is only in it for themselves and what they can get out of the partnership won't get the most out of it. But in a team where everyone supports each other and thinks about what they can offer to make it better, everyone benefits!

When to approach an agent

An agent can do a lot for an illustrator, but it's also worth asking yourself what you can do for an agency: what are you offering that they don't already have?

Many new illustrators see getting an agent as a shortcut to success: if they can just land representation, they'll finally be able to make good money, have a steady stream of work and relax into a stable creative career – but as we've seen, this isn't necessarily the case.

Bear in mind that the agent isn't the one making us a success, and neither are they responsible for that – they're simply there to help us on our journey. They can support us to improve and offer new opportunities, but they can't do the job for us. This is why an agency wants to know that a new artist can handle themselves professionally on their own first, by:

- Being able to find commissions on their own
- Completing projects with clients on time
- Presenting their work well.

The agent needs to see that an illustrator already has the drive and enthusiasm to make it into a serious career. These qualities, along with good technical skills and an interesting style (which we've already covered), are the entry test and application – without them, taking someone on would be a risk. An agency invests in its artists, and so it wants to be sure you're a good investment.

While you do need to reach a certain professional level by yourself to get an agent, their role is to support you. They won't be able to tell you what 'success' means to you or when you've 'made it' – and as much as they might encourage it, they can't make you work hard either! But they can help: be sure to tell them what you want for your career, and ask for assistance with whatever you need.

In short, agencies are excited to work with illustrators who:

- Have a few clients under their belt
- Have a couple of years' experience
- Can offer a unique style or specialist skill
- Have a solid work ethic
- Have proven themselves as a professional.

185

This offers them something they don't have – and want. If you can come armed with these things, it won't be a case of which agency might take you on; you'll be able to choose which one you want to partner with. Then, you can approach an agent on the same level both as potential business partners and as a professional ready to take your career to the next level, rather than someone who needs hand-holding.

Getting an agent too soon means missing out on all the valuable experiences that those early years of freelancing entail: it doesn't show an illustrator how to be independent, and they'll be completely reliant on their agent for work.

Taking the time to understand the business on your own for a few years will make you a better illustrator and businessperson. It'll give you more confidence in your abilities too.

Submit your work the right way

If you feel that you're ready to apply to an agency, then it's time to find a good fit for your work and personality.

Most of the time, a thoughtful email to the right person in an agency is enough to ensure your work is looked at and given fair consideration. However, because illustration agencies can receive hundreds of applications in a year, some have preferred methods of receiving them – and are very particular about it. If you don't follow the specific instructions that the agency outlines, your work might be discarded without ever being seen.

Every illustration agency publishes its submission guidelines on its website. These can be as simple as 'send an email to [agency email address]', or specific steps that they want applicants to follow. Submission guidelines might be hard to find, so if you do find yourself wanting to call or email an agency to ask what they are, just take a few more minutes to look carefully through its website. Agencies publish their guidelines online precisely so that a member of their team doesn't have to keep fielding these kinds of calls – so research this thoroughly, rather than making agency staff the first port of call. (See the Further resources section for a link to a blog post listing several well-known illustration agencies and their submission guidelines. Not every agency is listed, so do double check their guidelines before sending anything to ensure you have the most up-to-date information.)

Illustration agencies, particularly the smaller ones, aren't always actively looking to expand – so if you don't hear anything back, try again in a few months.

Introducing yourself to an agency

Good introductory emails

If you genuinely can't find submission guidelines on an illustration agency's website, defaulting to a well-considered and polite email to a specific, senior agency member is a good alternative.

Here's what to include:

- A short introduction to you: who and where you are
- A short background of your work history and any notable clients
- The reason why you're emailing – i.e. 'I would like to work with you'
- A link to your website and social media, if they want to see more
- Your contact details
- A small selection of your best illustrations appropriate for this particular agency.

The most important item by far on this list is the illustrations. Be sure to embed them directly in the email – not as attachments – so they can be seen immediately on opening. This means small enough file sizes to be suitable for sending over email, but not so small that image quality is reduced:

- .jpg or .png files between 1500px and 2000px (longest edge) saved for the web work well
- File sizes in .tiff or .psd files may be too large
- Sending layered .psd files or .ai files is unnecessary – a flattened image is ideal.

Avoid putting your illustrations behind a link, or in a folder or zip file – it doesn't show them effectively. Illustrations can grab attention in all sorts of contexts, so make sure to use yours to your advantage. They're what you'll be assessed on, as they serve to catch the recipient's eye and draw them into reading more.

Bad introductory emails

A good introductory email to an agent will be looked at: it might only be scanned quickly though, which is why it's so important to show your illustrations. They are what makes an agent or client stop in their tracks and examine the rest of the email, if they like what they see.

Take the following example of a bad one:

What's wrong with this picture?

- No images immediately visible
- No introductory text or additional information
- No links to the artist's website or social media.

– there's nothing here to catch an agent's attention. These things may be hidden away inside the .pdf or Word document – but if the agent is having a busy day, they aren't going to take the time to look all through these documents.

This email is addressed to four different agencies, which also shows a lack of effort on the illustrator's part: what might interest one agency won't necessarily interest another. The artist hasn't taken the time to look through each of their agency's submission guidelines and contact them individually. To put it bluntly, this is pretty lazy and unlikely to get a response – other than one (or more) of those agencies replying to ask the artist not to copy them into future emails.

Exercise: Write your own introduction email

We've already seen what a good introduction should include – and what a bad one looks like – so now it's time to write your own to keep for future use.

The example below will give you an idea of tone, length and content as a basic outline: but write this in your own words, make it specific to you and add your own personality to it.

This introduction is specifically for agents, but with some adjustment it could work for client introductions too. If you're sending an introduction to a client, you might want to direct yours more to the industry they work in, and make sure to show projects suitable for that sector.

Dear [Agent Name]

My name is [Name]. I'm an illustrator from [Country/City] and I'd love the opportunity to work with you.

I work in a [description of your] style that is easily adaptable to many different commercial subjects. I have added a few images you might like here, and you can see more in my portfolio: [Link to your website]

I've been working as an illustrator for a few years and I've worked with [Client 1], [Client 2] and [Client 3]. I feel I'm ready to take my career to the next level. I'd really appreciate any advice you might be able to offer.

I look forward to hearing from you.

Kind regards

[Name]
[Phone number]
[Website and social media links]

[image 1] [image 2] [image 3]

This email:

1. Addresses a specific person
2. Tells them who you are, where you're from and what you want
3. Gives them a short description of your work
4. Shows some of your work and offers a link to your website
5. Gives a clue to your work experience
6. Asks a question – in this case, asking for advice
7. Gives them your contact details and social media links.

If you want to engage with an agent or client and make a connection, asking for advice is a great first step. Even if they aren't able to represent or hire you right now, by asking them for some advice and returning a couple of months later, having demonstrated that you've followed it, you're building up trust and familiarity.

You don't necessarily need to ask an agent if they'd like to represent you. If you're an illustrator emailing an agent, that's a given – if your work is good enough to wow them, they'll bring it up!

Choosing an agency

Choosing the right business partner is crucial: pick the wrong one, and we might not achieve our goals; pick the right one, and we might surpass them!

While all agencies follow some broad standards, some are better than others – and not every agency is a good fit for every artist. You might try working with a few agencies before you find the one you get along with best.

Some illustrators are represented by different agencies at the same time: it's not uncommon for an artist to have an agent in their home country and another one for larger markets, distant time zones or different language-speaking territories. Many agencies prefer to represent artists globally; but, for example, if working with multiple agencies due to language barriers will benefit you, it's possible to negotiate this.

Ask the right questions

All agencies are different, and generally they don't communicate much with each other. Some agencies might excel in one area, but not in others. Before joining an agency, be sure to ask lots of questions and find out:

- Who you'll be working with
- What they do that other agencies don't
- What they're good at doing.

We might not have our pick of the top agencies while we're still in the process of establishing ourselves – but the first offer we get isn't always the best one we're likely to receive either. It's important to consider them carefully.

If the agency has any terms that you aren't happy with, try to negotiate them, as a good agent will respect you for doing that. If they're unwilling to bend, perhaps they aren't a good fit for you.

The Society of Artists Agents has a code of ethics for agents[35] that outlines what is considered fair practice. The organisation itself doesn't have many official member agencies, but others follow similar guidelines. You can use this code of ethics to guide your questions to any agency.

Choosing the right agency for you

What is true is that you'll always get mixed reviews of agencies. You might hear bad things about an agency from one artist and great things from another. Illustrators who have success with agents and work well with them will be positive; but understandably, others who've had bad experiences (or can't get an agent at all) might have negative feelings towards them.

Not every agent is right for every artist, regardless of how good or bad the agent or artist might be. I have great relationships with some illustrators and perhaps more challenging ones with others – sometimes it's just not a good fit! It's possible that you and your agent might have to work together for a while before this becomes clear – but that also

---

can be the case before a relationship blooms into a fruitful partnership. There's no harm in trying out an agency and seeing what happens (see the Further resources for a list of well-known agencies).

Selecting an agency checklist

If you're considering joining an agency, look for the following:

☐ Does it have a good reputation?

Email other artists that the agency represents to get some reviews.

☐ Where is it located?

This may not be as important as it once was, but an agency

operating from a bedroom in a small village might not have the

same opportunities as an agency in a big city.

☐ What territories does it cover?

Some are global, while others only operate in one country.

☐ How experienced is the agency – how long has it been running?

☐ What kind of client list does it have as a result?

☐ How big is it?

An agency doesn't need to be a big operation – but if one agent is

working with 30 artists, you won't get the attention you deserve.

☐ How and when are its artists paid?

☐ What's the commission rate, and does the agency charge any other fees?

☐ How will it market your work? Ask for specific methods.

☐ How does it market its other illustrators?

Are portfolios updated regularly, does the agency have a good social

media presence, and is it consistent in its efforts?

☐ What does it need from you – a selection of work, client list, personal information?

☐ Can you keep your existing clients?

After signing with an agent

As we've seen, if we're successful in getting an agent, that isn't the time to relax and wait for jobs to roll in: we're taking on a partner invested in our success who will share in the rewards (more on this in Chapter 16). If an illustrator takes their foot off the accelerator as soon as they join an agency, they're communicating that they aren't really a good partner; but if they keep working hard and bring enthusiasm to the job, their partner at the agency will too.

Your agent's responsibilities relate to your work with clients, so you'll need to:

- Organise your work and manage your own time
- Plan your career
- Stay motivated and engaged.

While your agent can definitely assist with these things, this is of course

your freelance business and, ultimately, your responsibility.

If you should feel that your agent isn't providing the help you need, always communicate openly and honestly: feel free to ask, rather than waiting for them to offer. If they can't support your career in the way you want, there's always the option of finding another agency able to do that instead. It's fine to have high expectations of an agent, but equally for them to expect you to give a lot in return too. An agent is more likely to invest time, money and effort into an illustrator who's eager to develop, willing to put in the work and open to their advice. It's a real pleasure to collaborate with an artist who's keen and wants to grow!

In the final chapter, we'll delve into what working with an agent actually looks like.

Key takeaways

- Consider what can you offer an agency.
- Check to see if your style fills a gap in what the agency already offers.
- An agency can help with your career, but ultimately you are responsible for it.
- Don't approach an agent too soon: wait until you've got some experience.
- Find the agency's submission guidelines to make sure your work is actually looked at.
- Write a great introductory email and include some images!
- Be honest with the agent, so they know how they can help you progress.
- Find out as much as you can about an agency before joining.

16

Working with an agent

Your agent is your business partner

For some freelance illustrators, their agent might be the closest thing they have to a co-worker for much of their career – maybe even a friend. An illustrator and their agent are on the same team, with a shared goal: if the illustrator isn't busy, the agent doesn't make any money, so it's in the agent's best interest to keep them in work.

The illustrator offers creative skills and the agent brings industry experience, business skills and a network of clients. As we saw in Chapter 15, you and your agent are, in a sense, business partners. If both are fulfilling their roles to the best of their ability, it's likely to be a good, happy and hopefully lucrative partnership!

Outsourcing work to an agent

As we've also seen, professional illustrators can outsource some of the non-creative parts of their job to an agent in the same way they might outsource their tax return to an accountant. If an illustrator wants to spend more time doing creative work, they need to do less of something else to make that time.

It's rare for one person to be naturally good at both creating and selling: these two roles require investment of time and expertise to do well. This is why agents exist: they know that creatives like to create and often don't want to do the other stuff. Their time is better spent making work than filling out forms for clients, reading contracts and chasing down late payment. And spending time deciphering legal agreements or keeping track of invoices isn't going to advance their career in the same way as working on their creative skills or expanding their portfolio.

Recognising our limitations is okay: we don't have to do everything ourselves as freelancers. We can make less progress in the creative part of our job if we do.

If we're incredibly skilled artists but have little or no interest in the business part, it's perfectly reasonable to focus on our strengths and what we do best. (That said, it's still important to be across some basics: we need to know enough to make sure we aren't being taken advantage of, and the difference between a good deal and a bad one.)

So far, we've seen that by the time we start working with an agent, we need to be at the point where we can already run our business solo. Rather than signing up with an agent because we can't do what they do, we recognise that they specialise in that part instead, while we're choosing to focus on our own talent. The team this creates works together well by allowing each person to maximise their individual strengths.

Outsourcing parts of your work to an agent means not only being able to do more of the work you enjoy, but which can have the biggest impact on your career: work that maximises your potential for bigger and better clients and projects.

How agents get you work

There are three main ways that agents supply illustrators with work:

- A client gets in touch with the agency to hire a specific artist – this is common for more established illustrators who have built up a following already.
- A client approaches the agency with a brief and asks for recommendations. It's much quicker and easier to ask an agent for a handful of suitable illustrators for a project, than it is to search the internet or social media for the right fit.
- The agency approaches clients with an artist's work to show it to the right people. Even if the client doesn't have a project at that time, the agent stays in touch with them to keep the illustrator's work fresh in their mind for when the right project comes along.

How agents are paid

Agents are paid by commission, which is a percentage of project fees (typically around 30%). This is an optimal payment model because if you're not working, you don't pay your agent anything: as a result, they want you to be busy and will do what they can to make that happen, since their own income depends on it. You're both working together towards the same goal.

Some agencies charge other optional fees for things they offer, such as different marketing opportunities; while other agencies even charge artists to put their portfolios on their websites, which is less optimal. If an agent wants to charge you a fee upfront before they've found you any work, you might want to keep looking for another one. Agencies can make money out of artists this way without finding them any work at all, which suggests that they don't have those artists' best interests as a priority.

If you don't want to pay a percentage of your fees to an agent, naturally that's fine – it just means you'll need to handle the other aspects of the job yourself. Some people find the service provided by an agent to be worth the cost, while others feel that the agent is taking money away from them rather than providing a valuable service.

You definitely don't need an agent to have a successful career, but getting to grips with all the other skills you'll need simply means that it might take more time to reach your goals.

Agents solve problems

Part of an agent's role is problem-solving: for any illustrator, there always will be unforeseen problems that might delay or derail a project. It's important to be open with an agent about what the issue is, so they have all the information they need to sort it out effectively.

For example, if we're facing a problem that means we can't meet a deadline or complete a project at all, it's important to share it with the agent and come up with a solution together. Two heads are better than one, and an experienced agent will have dealt with most commonplace problems many times before. (It's perhaps worth mentioning that an agent might have something to say about it, if it's an unprofessional or irresponsible issue that could have been avoided – but regardless, they will appreciate the honesty.)

The agent won't necessarily share everything with the client, but they can find a good solution when they know exactly what's needed.

Agents are human

Agents are human, with preferences, biases, strengths, weaknesses, feelings and insecurities. They might have a different skill set to a working illustrator, but they're not so different. They work in the same industry, and many have had a creative career at some point in the past. You can be sure they admire your creative skills and respect the work you do.

Agents make mistakes, and it's no more reasonable for you to expect them to be perfect than it is for them to expect you to be. If you can accept that both sides will make occasional mistakes but are trying their best, you can work together well. Support and forgive each other, as teammates should.

While an agency can handle many of the business aspects of an illustrator's work, it's also worth noting that treating it like a business and staying on top of your finances is key. Mistakes can happen with payment and other issues: it's important to stay informed about your livelihood, so any errors can be resolved quickly.

Work harder than your agent

You'll have put in a lot of hard work to get an agent, so now isn't the time to stop: keep going with all the great promotion and hustling you've been doing, as it can take a while for a new partnership to get up to full speed.

Some artists are busy from day one, but it often takes a few months for an illustrator's work to be introduced to the agency's clients and find opportunities that are a good fit – especially if they have a specialist style or skill set. As we saw in the previous chapter, if we were to take our foot off the gas and wait for the agent to find us projects, the partnership wouldn't be running as efficiently as it could.

When things are going smoothly, your agent sends you projects to work on. But in the early days or during quiet periods, aim to work harder than your agent in securing new commissions. This is your career, so of course it goes without saying that you'll be working hard at it anyway! But putting that bit of extra effort into self-promotion once you have an agent means they have to keep up with you too.

If they can see how much you're putting into your own self-promotion, they'll have to match that to justify their commission. If both you and the agency are working at 100% to develop your career, things will fall into place so much faster.

Go the extra mile

- Contact your own clients for more work, and find new clients to contact.
- Copy your agent into these emails, so they can see your determination.
- Send your agent a list of clients you'd like to work for but can't reach yourself. (This is a great way to give the agent some specific areas on which to focus.)
- Ask your agent for a portfolio review and to set you a project to expand and improve it.

Make your agent prove their commitment to your success: usually, this is something that artists don't do when they join an agency. They might be too hesitant or unsure to express clearly what they want from their agent, but an agency works with artists with all kinds of personalities. They're very used to lack of confidence in new artists, and a good agent encourages them to develop it. They'll appreciate your curiosity and eagerness!

If you give your agent a list of clients you want to work with, they'll make their best effort to contact them: it's proactive, and shows initiative. Then you can ask the agent next month if they've been in touch with those clients – this should really motivate them to put in the effort.

Work harder than your agent and make them work hard for you, and you'll both get the most out of the relationship.

Build the relationship with your agent

Agencies have a lot of artists to look after, so they can't give their full attention to every one at the same time. This isn't for any nefarious or spiteful reasons; simply that they naturally pay more attention to the illustrators who are the busiest, most enthusiastic and with whom they have the best working relationship.

In an ideal world, all of an agency's artists would be equally busy and it would spread its efforts evenly; but the busiest artists need more attention, the most enthusiastic artists ask for more attention, and the nicest and friendliest artists get more attention because it's a more pleasant experience to interact with them.

If you feel that your agent isn't doing their best work for you, talk to them: ask how you can help make things better, and tell them what you want from them. Give them more work they can use to market you, stay in touch often and build the relationship.

Give a lot and expect a lot

Joining an agency can take your career to a new level, if you maximise your efforts and capitalise on the opportunity, step up your game and demand the best from yourself and your agent.

By giving a lot to your agency, you can ask for a lot in return. By doing the things discussed in this chapter, such as:

- Regularly supplying your agent with new work
- Supporting other artists
- Asking what the agency needs from you
- Demonstrating enthusiasm and commitment to the partnership

– you have every right to demand the same level of effort and commitment from the agency. You can ask them for advice on your portfolio and for their time and attention; you can also justifiably query why they haven't found you any work, if you have a slow period.

You're fulfilling your part of the bargain – they should too.

Trust each other

The best teamwork happens where there's respect and trust: if an illustrator is taking work behind their agent's back and cutting them out of deals, the agent will find out eventually and no longer trust them. Equally, if an agent isn't being upfront with the illustrator about how they're marketing their work, or is failing to be open about financial matters, it's not exactly unreasonable to suspect they might not have the artist's best interests at heart.

In the conversations I've shared with many illustrators, I've rarely heard anything alarmingly negative: agencies with bad business practices don't tend to last long. Approach your relationship with an agent with openness, and assume the best. Be proud of your agency and of being part of the team. Just as your agency wants you to succeed, want success for them too.

Everyone wins!

Key takeaways

- Your agent is your business partner.
- Agents make mistakes just like everyone else!
- Demand a lot from your agent and give a lot back.
- You decide where you want your career to go – the agency helps.
- Work harder than your agent so they have to keep up.
- Be open and honest with your agent, and expect the same in return.

Final thoughts

Many illustrators let fear and setbacks hold them back from becoming exceptional. They're too scared to stand out or risk failure. Those illustrators find it increasingly difficult to have a career in the creative field they love.

The ones who can overcome challenges, think strategically, commit themselves to the work and ignore distractions will be easily identifiable in the future. Whenever you see a beautifully effective illustrated advertising campaign, bestselling book or the world's top brands using illustration, they'll have been worked on by exceptionally skilled creatives: 'pretty good' won't get the chance to work on these kinds of projects.

Pushing yourself to aim higher, learn more and practise deliberately is difficult and uncomfortable: but that discomfort is what keeps most illustrators from being truly outstanding at what they do.

Throughout this book we've explored some of the common challenges that new illustrators face, and how they can be reframed and used to your advantage. We've discovered that being a beginner is a good thing, and that passion and inspiration are by-products of doing the work, rather than the sources of great art. We've also discussed the mindful use of procrastination. By developing the right mindset from the start and using your time and resources effectively, you can overcome these challenges and become an exceptional creative.

We've looked at some of the people you'll interact with in your professional career: peers, teachers, agents and clients, and how making the most of these relationships can help you thrive as a freelancer. And we've taken a more practical look into some of the skills and habits which can transform you from an enthusiastic beginner into a valued professional collaborator that clients trust and respect.

Becoming a seasoned professional takes time, but knowing what it entails means you can start practising and refining those skills early.

Share what you know

As you continue to progress in your creative journey and grow as an illustrator, there'll come a point where you'll have the opportunity to pay it forward and contribute to the industry. You don't have to be an expert to share valuable information with others; you just need to know something they might find helpful.

Sharing your knowledge with others about what you've discovered not only fosters a sense of collaboration and community within the illustration industry, but also contributes to your own growth as an artist. By sharing your work, methods, ideas and enthusiasm for illustration, you can help elevate the industry for everyone while improving your own skills and building your personal brand.

One of the most enriching things an experienced artist can do is to inspire and help others achieve their creative goals.

Before we wrap this up, remember that starting up any new venture can be overwhelming. However, armed with the knowledge and insights shared in this book, you have the ability to launch your creative career.

Now it's time to go make some work and show it to people!

I hope you've enjoyed reading this book and continue to find it useful in building your new career. You're on a path full of possibilities, and I'd love to hear about your journey and experiences as an illustrator.

If you'd like to get in touch, email me at: theillustratorsguide@ gmail.com, and if you'd like to join The Illustrator's Guide community, visit: www.theillustratorsguide.com.

Further resources

Books

Sönke Ahrens (2022) *How to Take Smart Notes: One Simple Technique to Boost Writing, Learning and Thinking*, Amazon KDP.

Derek Brazell and Jo Davies (2017) *Becoming a Successful Illustrator*, Bloomsbury Visual Arts.

Derek Brazell and Jo Davies (2023) *Getting Illustration Clients*, Bloomsbury Visual Arts.

James Clear (2018) *Atomic Habits: An Easy and Proven Way to Build Good Habits and Break Bad Ones*, Random House Business.

Jim Collins (2001) *Good to Great: Why Some Companies Make the Leap... and Others Don't*, Random House.

Lisa Congdon (2014) *Art, Inc. The Essential Guide for Building Your Career as an Artist*, Chronicle Books.

Lisa Congdon (2019) *Find Your Artistic Voice: The Essential Guide to Working Your Creative Magic*, Chronicle Books.

Holly DeWolf (2009) *Breaking into Freelance Illustration: A Guide for Artists, Designers and Illustrators*, How Books.

Allan Dib (2018) *The 1-Page Marketing Plan: Get New Customers, Make More Money, and Stand Out from the Crowd*, Page Two.

Joe Fig (2009) *Inside the Painter's Studio*, Princeton Architectural Press.

Martina Flor (2020) *The Big Leap: A Guide to Freelancing for Creatives*, Princeton Architectural Press.

Malcolm Gladwell (2009) *Outliers: The Story of Success*, Penguin.

Seth Godin (2018) *Linchpin: Are you Indispensable? How to Drive Your Career and Create a Remarkable Future*, Piatkus.

Seth Godin (2020) *The Practice: Shipping Creative Work*, Penguin Business.

Graphic Artists Guild (2021) *The Graphic Artists Guild Handbook: Pricing & Ethical Guidelines*, 16th edition, MIT Press.

Morgan Housel (2020) *The Psychology of Money: Timeless Lessons on Wealth, Greed and Happiness*, Harriman House.

Chase Jarvis (2019) *Creative Calling: Establish a Daily Practice,*

Infuse Your World with Meaning and Succeed in Work + Life, Harper Business.

Leif Kendall (2011) *Brilliant Freelancer: Discover the Power of Your Own Success*, Pearson Business.

Austin Kleon (2012) *Steal Like an Artist: 10 Things Nobody Told You about Being Creative*, Workman Publishing.

Austin Kleon (2014) *Show Your Work: 10 Ways to Share Your Creativity and Get Discovered*, Workman Publishing.

Jake Knapp and John Zeratsky (2018) *Make Time: How to Focus on What Matters Every Day*, Bantam Press.

Meg Mateo Ilasco and Joy Cho (2010) *Creative Inc. The Ultimate Guide to Running a Successful Freelance Business*, Chronicle Books.

Mike Michalowicz (2012) *The Pumpkin Plan: A Simple Strategy to Grow a Remarkable Business in any Field*, Penguin Portfolio.

Cal Newport (2016) *Deep Work: Rules for Focused Success in a Distracted World*, Piatkus.

Cal Newport (2016) *So Good They Can't Ignore You: Why Skills Trump Passion in the Quest for Work You Love*, Piatkus.

Steven Pressfield (2002) *The War of Art: Break through the Blocks and Win Your Inner Creative Battles*, Warner Books.

Steven Pressfield (2012) *Turning Pro: Tap Your Inner Power and Create Your Life's Work*, Black Irish Entertainment.

Darrell Rees (2014) *How to Be an Illustrator*, Laurence King Publishing.

Rick Rubin (2023) *The Creative Act: A Way of Being*, Canongate Books.

Simon Stern (2008) *The Illustrator's Guide to Law and Legal Practice*, Association of Illustrators.

Ben Tallon (2015) *Champagne and Wax Crayons: Riding the Madness of the Creative Industry*, LID Publishing.

Podcasts

Building Your Brand, with Liz Mosley
Deep Questions, with Cal Newport
Inside Illustration, by the Association of Illustrators
Martina Flor's Open Studio
Mimi, with Melanie Johnsson

The Chase Jarvis Live Show
The Creative Condition Podcast
The Futur, with Chris Do
The Handsome Frank Illustration Podcast
Thoughts on Illustration, with Tom Froese

Online resources

Learning platforms

CreativeLive: www.creativelive.com – all kinds of top-quality creative classes.
Domestika www.domestika.org – big focus on illustration.
Skillshare: www.skillshare.com – for design and visual arts.
Udemy: www.udemy.com – business and professional skills.

Professional societies

Association of Illustrators (AOI): https://theaoi.com – the professional body for illustrators based in the UK, with members everywhere.
Graphic Arts Guild: https://graphicartistsguild.org/resources – resources and information for illustrators.
Society of Artists Agents: https://saahub.com/ethics – code of ethics.

Legal and licensing

Artquest: https://artquest.org.uk/artlaw – legal information and email help for your art practice.
Association of Illustrators: https://theaoi.com/resources/contracts/illustrator-commissioner-agreement/ – the AOI's commissioning agreement (for members only).
DACS: www.dacs.org.uk/knowledge-base – legal and licensing help for artists.

Blogs

Business of Illustration: http://businessofillustration.com – blog with many useful articles for freelance illustrators.
The Illustrator's Guide: https://theillustratorsguide.com – my blog with links to the YouTube channel and more.

YouTube channels

Alexandra Helm – @AlexandraHelm
Anoosha Syed – @AnooshaSyed
Art Business with Ness – @ArtBusinesswithNess
Emma Carpenter Illustration – @EmmaCarpenterIllustration
Fran Meneses – @FranMeneses
Holly Exley – @hollyexley
Kendyll Hillegas – @KendyllHillegas
Mr Tom Froese – @TomFroese
The Illustrator's Guide – @TheIllustratorsGuide

Illustration agencies

A selection of agencies from around the world I've had good experiences with, or about which I've heard good things:
Agent 002: www.agent002.com
Agent Pekka: https://agentpekka.com
Anna Goodson: www.agoodson.com
B&A Reps: www.ba-reps.com
Central Illustration Agency: https://centralillustration.com
Closer & Closer: www.closerandcloser.co
Colagene Paris: www.colageneparis.com/en
Creasenso: www.creasenso.com/en
Debut Art: www.debutart.com
Folio Art: https://folioart.co.uk
Handsome Frank: www.handsomefrank.com
Heart Agency: www.heartagency.com
Illustration X: www.illustrationx.com
Jelly: www.thisisjelly.com/uk
JSR: www.jsragency.com
Lemonade Illustration Agency: www.lemonadeillustration.com

Meiklejohn: www.meiklejohn.co.uk
NB Illustration: www.nbillustration.co.uk
Pocko: www.pocko.com
Snyder NY: https://wearesnyder.com/us
Studio Pi: https://studiopi.co.uk
The Artworks: www.theartworksinc.com
The Bright Agency: https://thebrightagency.com/uk
The Jacky Winter Group: https://jackywinter.com

The Illustrator's Guide list of various agencies' submission guidelines:
https://theillustratorsguide.com/illustration-agency-submissions
Partfaliaz directory of illustration agencies: www.partfaliaz.com/illus-tration-agencies-directory

Acknowledgements

First and foremost, I would like to thank Nicholas Dawe, the founder of Folio illustration agency, who took a chance on an inexperienced but enthusiastic aspiring agent. Also, the rest of the team at Folio: Kim Meech, Peter Henderson, Lizzie Lomax, Katie Wade, David Barrett and Jill Smith, who keep me regularly supplied with new ideas. A big thank you goes to the incredible illustrators I work with every day at Folio.

I would also like to thank the many early readers who gave me feedback on the first draft of this book. Thank you to Michael Parkin for the great interior illustrations and Tom Etherington for the cover design.

Although he won't remember me, Peter Norris taught a short business class in my illustration course at university and sparked a genuine interest in this part of the industry, which changed the course of my career. (Additionally, an apology to the rest of my lecturers for not giving my best effort then. Just know that it did finally sink in!)

I'd like to thank George Warren, who I met while doing stand-up comedy in London. Since then, George has been my friend, professional coach and a valuable sounding board for all kinds of ideas. His encouragement has pushed me to achieve so many personal and professional goals.

Finally, I'd like to thank all the authors and podcasters I love, who will likely never know I exist, but who have opened my mind to all the world has to offer.

About the author

James Hughes is an illustrator's agent at Folio illustration agency. He began writing articles and recording videos for aspiring illustrators in 2017, and has contributed to the Association of Illustrators as a contract adviser and writer.

James has a BA degree in Illustration from the University of Huddersfield. Before becoming an agent, he worked as a freelance illustrator; he now coaches and mentors new illustrators, and gives talks to university students.

A serial hobbyist, James has dabbled in stand-up comedy, martial arts, magic, macro photography, cooking (and eating). He lives in Yorkshire.

The Illustrator's Guide is his first book.

Printed in the USA
CPSIA information can be obtained
at www.ICGtesting.com
LVHW091334201123
764439LV00004B/25